TRANSFORMING BODIES

Transforming Bodies: Gendered Stories of Embodied Change provides unique and original research on gendered bodies. It explores the ways that bodies transform and change, and how these transformations relate to the intersections of gender, race, body shape, names, age, dis/ability, activism, performance, and beyond.

Combining personal narratives, sociological theories, and artistic representations, this book dives into questions on transformation and change, such as: "How do we understand our bodies as transformative places? What does it mean to exist in a body that is consistently questioned? Are our embodiments always in some state(s) of change?"

The book contains original stories on embodied transformation and includes creative engagement by using commissioned art to represent various forms of transformation and change. Each chapter has a comprehensive list of key words and questions for reflection and discussion.

Transforming Bodies: Gendered Stories of Embodied Change is an accessible book that will be engaging for both students and scholars, as well as those outside of academia with an interest in body politics, gender, race, disability, and activism.

Victoria Kannen is Professor of Sociology at Cambrian College in Ontario, Canada. She is the author of *Gendered Bodies and Public Scrutiny: Women's Stories of Staring, Strangers, and Fierce Resistance* (2021). She is also the co-editor of *Virtual Identities and Digital Culture* (2023).

TRANSFORMING BODIES

Gendered Stories of Embodied Change

Victoria Kannen

LONDON AND NEW YORK

Designed cover image: Damian Mellin

First published 2025
by Routledge
4 Park Square, Milton Park, Abingdon, Oxon OX14 4RN

and by Routledge
605 Third Avenue, New York, NY 10158

Routledge is an imprint of the Taylor & Francis Group, an informa business

© 2025 Victoria Kannen

The right of Victoria Kannen to be identified as author of this work has been asserted in accordance with sections 77 and 78 of the Copyright, Designs and Patents Act 1988.

All rights reserved. No part of this book may be reprinted or reproduced or utilised in any form or by any electronic, mechanical, or other means, now known or hereafter invented, including photocopying and recording, or in any information storage or retrieval system, without permission in writing from the publishers.

Trademark notice: Product or corporate names may be trademarks or registered trademarks, and are used only for identification and explanation without intent to infringe.

British Library Cataloguing-in-Publication Data
A catalogue record for this book is available from the British Library

Library of Congress Cataloging-in-Publication Data
Names: Kannen, Victoria, 1981– author.
Title: Transforming bodies : gendered stories of embodied change / Victoria Kannen.
Description: Abingdon, Oxon ; New York, NY : Routledge, 2025. | Includes bibliographical references and index.
Identifiers: LCCN 2024029431 (print) | LCCN 2024029432 (ebook) | ISBN 9781032460949 (hbk) | ISBN 9781032460932 (pbk) | ISBN 9781003380061 (ebk)
Subjects: LCSH: Gender identity. | Change (Psychology)
Classification: LCC HQ1075 .K354 2025 (print) | LCC HQ1075 (ebook) | DDC 305.3—dc23/eng/20240820
LC record available at https://lccn.loc.gov/2024029431
LC ebook record available at https://lccn.loc.gov/2024029432

ISBN: 978-1-032-46094-9 (hbk)
ISBN: 978-1-032-46093-2 (pbk)
ISBN: 978-1-003-38006-1 (ebk)

DOI: 10.4324/9781003380061

Typeset in Sabon
by Apex CoVantage, LLC

CONTENTS

Preface — vii
Acknowledgments — viii

1   Bodies — 1

    Thinking It Through 2
    Gendered Bodies 4
    Stories 6
    Participants 9
    The Author 13
    Stories + Art 13
    Book Structure 15

2   Intersections — 20

    Intersectionality 24
    Race 27
    Sexuality and Queerness 31

3   Shapes — 36

    Normal Bodies 39
    Larger Bodies + Smaller Bodies 40
    Body Positivity 43
    Transformed Chests 46
    Body Neutrality 50

vi Contents

4   Ages and Dis/Abilities   53

We Are All Ageist 56
Dis/Ability and Explorations of Self 60
Lives, Interrupted 62

5   Names   68

Pronouns Are Political 70
Being Trans, Changing Names 73
Being Political, Changing Names 77
Names That We Get to Choose 80

6   Performances   83

Hair 86
Fashion 89
Tattoos 93
We All Perform 96

7   Bodies Transform   98

Bodies as Homes 99
Bodies as Shared 101
Bodies as In-Between Places 105
Bodies Have Stories 108

Index   *119*

PREFACE

This is a book about bodies and the ways that they transform. It is intended for those who may be new to reading academic books on the subject or simply for those of you who want to add to your knowledge by way of theory and storytelling. This is not an all-encompassing textbook, but rather it is intended to be an accessible introduction to some complex ideas about changes that our bodies go through. In my last book, *Gendered Bodies and Public Scrutiny: Women's Stories of Staring, Strangers, and Fierce Resistance* (2021), I explored the ways that some women's bodies inspire awe, are considered odd, and experience a variety of scrutiny from the public. The stories in that book are complimentary to the stories in this one.

I'm so grateful that you wanted to read this book. I know that you might read it over the course of a few hours, a few days, a few months, or even a few years. In that time, your body will change. You will age – that one may be obvious – but you will also experience new things, new people, and new ideas that will impact how, where, and when you read this. Your body is changing right now. We all continually transform, but the idea of transformation is expansive and, sometimes, hard to grasp or accept. Transformation is something that often scares people. It can be frightening to imagine that some element(s) of who we are becoming might be unfamiliar.

It is my hope that the stories and thinking in this book will show you – in a less intimidating way – the variety of forms that transformation can take and that we can embrace those changes and, often, thrive because of them. Thank you for being open to these ideas.

ACKNOWLEDGMENTS

This book came together because of many wonderful people. I feel so much gratitude to the 14 participants who shared so much with me: their transformative insight, difficult memories, empowering ideas, laughter, and time. This book took the shape that it did because of their direction. I want to thank Damian Mellin. Damian is a wonderful person to go on a creative journey with. Damian's artistic direction for the book adds so much insight and this book looks and feels the way it does because of our fun, silly, and vibrant collaboration. Thanks to Charlotte Taylor and Jodie Collins for their editorial support and patience (!) through this project. Thank you to my beautiful partner in this life, Aaron. He unwaveringly supports every single thing I want to work on. I am grateful for him, every day. Thank you to our children. Whether the three of you have read this far into the book or not, I love you forever. Lastly, thank you to all the people who will take some time to read this. I hope that these stories and ideas add something to your understanding of the messy, interesting, challenging, empowering, resistive, tough, and fun experiences that so many people's bodies go through.

1
BODIES

Introducing *Transforming Bodies*

FIGURE 1.1   Imagine how this image might relate to what is to come. This image is discussed in more detail within Chapter 1.

Damian Mellin, 2024

2 Transforming Bodies

Bodies change. Bodies transition. Bodies transform. These are realities that we all know, but some changes, transitions, and transformations are socially expected and (mostly) accepted, while others are feared and often reviled. Bodies are complicated and what happens to them over the course of a lifetime is difficult, if not impossible, to summarize.

Think of your body right now. What has it been through? What has been challenging for your body to deal with? What questions have other people had about your body? How might you imagine the ways that your body will change in the future?

This is a book about how bodies **transform**. More specifically, this is a book about how people talk about their bodily transformations. It is also a book that combines body stories with sociological theories that help explain them. It's my aim that when you read or listen to these words, you will gain some new understanding of what is possible for bodily change. Some of these changes we desire, some we try to ignore, and some we dread.

The stories that you will read here come from those who have grappled with transformation and want to share their insights with you. These insights are not the totality of who they are, of course. But our bodies are also not separate from who we are as people; they are the vessels through which we exist. When our physical being is undergoing change, it can be unsettling to our sense of self and how those around us understand and relate to us. So our goal here – together – is to work through ideas that challenge why transformation is so hard to talk about. Through their stories, some people in this book share how their lives were saved by their willingness to transform. However, some transformations were unwanted, and so these people share their stories to shed light and hopefully encourage you to learn from their experiences.

It is brave to talk about our bodies. It is brave to think about what is happening to them, what might happen to them, and what has happened to them. Our physical bodies also have a beginning and an end. Some of us believe that everything that transpires in our life exists within our bodies, while others believe that we might live on in some form after our physical bodies end. Regardless of how you frame your embodied existence, our bodies have stories to tell.

You'll notice that I talk directly to you throughout this book. As a professor, I always want to acknowledge that we are both involved in this process – I am the writer, but you are here as the reader. We shouldn't be too abstracted from each other. I'll introduce myself more formally later, but I just wanted to let you know that I'm aware that this kind of direct and conversational tone might seem unusual at first.

Thinking It Through

There are some complexities to thinking about how our bodies transform. We all seem to have different ideas about what it can mean for our bodies to actually *transform*. So, defining transformation is both very important and also quite abstract. For example, we can define 'transformation' in two general ways:

Transformation can represent a complete change in the appearance or character of something or someone. Typically, it is a word used to refer to a process in which a thing or person is improved in some way.

OR

Transformation is referred to as an act, process, or instance of transforming or being transformed.

If we look at the first definition, it focuses on the visual or character aspects of something that is transformed and/or improved. The second definition refers to transformation as a process. These are important to consider together. Transformation is a process of transforming some*thing*. So, then, what does it *actually* mean to transform?

When you look up the word *transform*, you will see the word *change* paired with it. Definitions of the word *transform* tend to look something like this:

a. to change in composition or structure
b. to change the outward form or appearance of
c. to change in character or condition

Okay, then to transform is to change.

The idea of 'change' is technically a neutral one, but the ways that people discuss change as it relates to our bodies is almost never neutral, unless it is intentionally crafted that way. Change is one of those ideas some people embrace (Change is good!), while others use it in order to unsettle (Change is hard!). In this book, you will hear stories from people who identify themselves as undergoing change in the form of **embodied transformation**. Embodied transformation sounds very technical, but we will use it to refer to the realities of how our bodies transform and the meanings that those transformations can have – both for ourselves and for others.

Their stories will speak to transformation through:

- intersections that consider the ways that race, sexuality, and gender intersect and intertwine
- shapes where we explore body sizes and their changes over time
- ages and dis/abilities which explore these realities as transformative experiences
- our names and how they can change because of gender, activism, and so on

4 Transforming Bodies

- our bodies and how they perform via fashion, tattooing, and/or hair, as well as and the ways that these are elements of personal expression and transformation

Gendered Bodies

The subtitle of the book is *Gendered Stories of Embodied Change*. The transformations you will learn about go way beyond gendered changes alone. So, why frame this as a discussion of gendered bodies? **Gender** is the undercurrent through which we identify ourselves from infancy. Even those who try to disrupt strict notions of gender are still positioned in relation to common understandings of gender that circulate in the world around us. Gendered ideas can feel inescapable, and so, when I am teaching, this is the topic on bodies that I tend to start with.

Before we explore gendered bodies, let's talk bodies. The **body** is a complicated idea. As Susie Orbach says, "[b]odies are and always have been shaped according to the specific cultural moment. There has never been a 'natural' body: a time when bodies were untainted by cultural practices" (2009, 165). We have a body and, to some extent, are our body. What does that mean? Well, our physical body is what keeps us alive, but our embodied experiences are what forms our relationships and adds significance to our lives. Again, let's think about our bodies right now. What has it accomplished today? What has it accomplished biologically? What has it accomplished socially?

Embodiment can be defined as the way we are located in a particular place and time and how these locations come to mean something socially – to us and other people (Richardson and Locks 2014). Some examples of our locations are the physical geographical location that we are in and the digital spaces we occupy, but this is also referring to our identities, such as our gender, race, age, abilities, sexuality, and so on. Our bodies are the space and place of all that transpires in life, from our birth until our death (Kannen 2021).

A key theory to understanding how bodies are social creations is through what's called the **constructionist approach**. This theory tells us that if we look at the things in our lives, they themselves do not have meaning, but we construct meaning for these things using systems of representation, such as language. We name things. The name and the thing are not connected in any intrinsic way, but it is through language that the way we represent things comes to be seen as 'normal' or natural. The key idea in this is 'construct'; to construct something means to build or create it. The constructionist approach does not prioritize 'things' as having natural qualities, rather it explores how these qualities are taught, learned, and reproduced through social interactions and relations. In this way, we can define representation in terms of how we create and produce meanings that we then give to things through the use of language.

Now, to gender. Gender is a structural idea in culture and the major undercurrent connecting all the participants in this book. It is not a biological identity, but rather, it is a social one – a constructed one. Gender refers to the socially constructed roles, behaviors, activities, and attributes that relate to understandings of masculinities, femininities, and non-binary identities in any given society. "Our indoctrination . . . begins before we are even born. From gender reveal parties to color-coded baby showers, society compels our allegiance to strict gender and sexual roles before our first breath" (Taylor 2021, 115). In Western societies, gender is also frequently understood as a binary; if one is masculine, one cannot, by definition, also take on the attributes of femininity. In other words, value and status may be afforded to one gender more than the other, and these advantages are sometimes gained at the expense of the other. The reason that I said earlier that identities, such as **non-binary**, are still related to gendered ideas, is because we can't understand being non-binary without acknowledging the binary itself.

Despite the existence of rules about gender, most of us can think of many examples where those rules are contradicted, including within our own experiences. For example, I am a woman who is much taller than my partner, who is a cisgender man. This is unusual, as straight or heterosexual couples tend to have the man's body taller than the woman's. The reason for this is because of the expectations of masculinity and femininity embedded in our bodies, such as a man's taller height implying authority, leadership, protection, and so on. We tend to know that these ideas are constructed, but our culture also tends to uphold them as if they are a rule. So, instead of saying masculinity or femininity, it is important to pluralize them – masculinities and femininities, since my partner is still very masculine, he is simply breaking a gendered rule in relation to me.

Defining gender strictly in terms of a singular masculinity or femininity is a problematic suggestion as it implies that only two, separate and discrete, gender categories exist. Here, we could discuss the ways in which people can identify as **cisgender** (cis), **transgender** (trans), **agender**, **genderless**, **genderfluid**, and certainly in other ways that have yet to be commonly defined. One aspect of the complexity of gender talk stems from the ways in which understandings of gender are understood to be natural: "Gender difference . . . is largely culturally constructed, yet appears entirely natural" (DeMello 2014, 118). What we expect our gendered bodies to do, how they behave, what they will produce, and how they will appear is often presumed to occur naturally. When that naturalness is disrupted or transformed, that is when things get more complicated.

What I ask of you, is that you think of gender as more like a verb than a noun or an adjective – we all 'do' gender, embedding it in the way we relate

6 Transforming Bodies

to other people. As I write these words, I am 'doing' gender – my hair is long, my nails are painted, my sweatpants are pink, my earrings are hoops (quite the look!). Individually, these elements do not necessarily 'read' as woman, but they are markers of femininity. Combined together, all of what I am doing speaks to how I want people to read my gendered body. It is much better to think of gender as a 'process.' Here, we are going to understand gender in its interactions in everyday life – through how people communicate and act with each other. If you consider what you do to prepare your body for the day, there are choices that you are expected to make to affirm the gender that you present with. Fashion. Hair. Make up (or no makeup). Jewelry. These choices convey some markers of gender within them. Some people use these markers to fulfill gendered expectations; some people use them to resist gendered expectations. Either way, we live in a world where gender is always a process and this process changes over the course of our lives.

Stories

In our daily lives, we tell people stories. We recount something that just happened, something that happened years ago, or something we thought might or should happen but maybe never did. We tell stories of our elders, our children, stories that were passed down to us, and stories we hope will be passed down to others. In a book called *True Reconciliation: How to be a Force for Change* by Jody Wilson-Raybould (2002) on truth and reconciliation for Indigenous peoples in Canada, she says, "When I think of truth, I think of storytelling. It is through stories that various truths are revealed in my culture, and in many Indigenous cultures" (33). To me, a non-Indigenous woman, I also see storytelling as a fundamental source of truth, especially when so many stories have been ignored, erased, and denied because their truth was so powerful, disruptive, or damaging. Here, I hope to provide a venue to give space and learning to stories that are often overlooked.

The stories collected for this book are from people who self-identified as experiencing bodily transformation. In looking for participants to interview, I put a call for participants out on Twitter (before it was called X) in 2023 (see Figure 1.2).

It was my intention to connect with people who have thoughtfully reflected on their transformations and were eager to share those experiences. I was grateful that nearly twenty people – mostly strangers – responded with interest in having me, and you, hear about their embodied transformations. Stories of change are not easy, and some people who reached out with interest in being a part of this project then changed their mind prior to our interview, which is completely understandable due to the personal and (potentially) stressful nature of these types of conversations. These are not all-encompassing narratives, rather these are stories told by particular people, all living in Canada and the United States,

Victoria Kannen's tweet

FIGURE 1.2

Victoria Kannen 2023

about their specific bodies. In all, there are 14 stories spread throughout the book – some are more featured than others because of the types of stories and reflections that they offer, but they all add important value to this book.

This book uses **qualitative methodology**. I chose to use semistructured, audio-recorded interviews in order to create a foundation for your learning. The use of interviews allows me to explore the participants' perceptions in a manner that can most effectively illustrate how they consider their body, how they understand transformation, how they self identify, and so on. I see the role of storytelling in this way to be a **feminist** practice as I create space for people to share their elements of their life in their own words and base my writing in coordination with their ideas on their lived experience. In my work, I strive to prioritize the lives and stories of people who identify as women, trans, and non-binary people.

The strategy to include personal narratives of our bodies is important for a number of reasons. First, these reflections are the moments that allow you as a reader to connect with examples that come from diverse perspectives. As the person writing this book, I want to position myself so that you know who I am, but only briefly. If the voice of this book was mostly my own, then the **privilege** that I experience as a white, cisgender, settler, able-bodied, tall woman is overshadowing the plethora of voices that can speak to how

8 Transforming Bodies

embodiments exist in these transformative ways. While my role in creating this should not be overlooked, I also don't want the privileges embedded in my story to overshadow the narratives you read going forward. Don't worry, though, my story will be scattered throughout. Second, this is an element of accessible learning. The inclusion of conversations is important because it breaks from more traditional theory which can be intimidating to students and those readers outside of academia. So, creating new research on the subject of bodies is vital. When teaching courses on bodies and embodiment, it is often difficult to find books that think through bodies without being too geared to one element of identity – such as gender or race – or texts that generally focus on embodied extremes, such as radical body modification.

I prefaced every interview that I conducted with complete transparency for the participants through an informed consent letter. The interviews were directed by the participants in the form of storytelling. I would only ask questions for clarification and interest, and the participants could choose not to answer any or all of them, and they were able to remove themselves from the project within 6 months of our interview. The interviews generally lasted between 1 and 2 hours. Some were emotional, while some were much more relaxed. They all were compelling and worthy of sharing here.

In all honesty, I took some time to grapple with how to properly tell these stories. I was reminded of this quote by Susie Orbach as I prepared to write this. She says that "[i]n the worst of cases, we may not feel that our bodies really belong to us – we will look at them as though from the outside, as a project we have to work on" (Orbach 2009, 51). I, in no way, want to frame these narratives as body projects as if they are laborious to us, but rather as points of reflection. It is such a privilege to be trusted with narratives – at times, very intimate, difficult narratives – of people's lives. It is so important to properly articulate these stories that I needed to take a few months in order to figure out how to best relay them. My method in what follows might seem a bit unorthodox, but perhaps the way I am writing this now is also unorthodox. The stories you will read are not entirely cohesive. They are 'snippets' of each discussion best suited for the direction that the book is taking. I chose this method because the stories were shared in nonlinear ways. Stories told through memories, contradictions, retractions, corrections, addendums, and anecdotes are rarely told from start to finish. All these people are still in the process of reflecting on their transformation and you will hear their thoughts woven throughout the entirety of this book.

The stories are the words taken from the interviewees themselves. I've tidied up the grammar and the occasional word choice, because when we are talking, we interrupt ourselves, switch gears and thoughts mid-sentence, and interrupt each other. This would be challenging to read, so I have edited minor elements to translate our discussion into readable text, but, otherwise, these are their stories, told through their own words.

These are the names you will see: Alane, Amelia, Anne, Ari, Audrey, Haz, Hila, Jasmine, Jules, Laura, Maria, Michelle, Ra'anaa, and Rachel. Ari, Haz, Laura, Maria, and Ra'anaa are not pseudonyms. These people wanted to use their own names to speak from their own experience, and to identify with the names that connect with who they are. The other participants chose the name listed here to act as a pseudonym. Every person has honored us by sharing their story and I am so glad you have decided to read/listen to them now.

Participants

Here is a brief description of each of the participants – sometimes using their own words – to provide some valuable context as you begin down this path.

Alane

When Alane was in her mid-40s she was diagnosed with breast cancer and was working as a secretary at a recycling center. In the years that have passed, Alane finds herself in her 50s, having recently earned her PhD. Her story explores her bodily changes, her outlook on life, and the impact that health has on influencing her ideas about identity.

Amelia

In her mid-50s, Amelia is over a decade cancer-free. Amelia's story focuses on the role that her experience with cancer has had on her body, her identities, and the way she now conceptualizes herself – as a woman, partner, and mother. She says,

> I've lost my hair. I lost all my eyebrows. And as you can see, it has never grown back. So, I only have eyebrows, I only have about a third of my eyelashes back. And they'll probably never come back. My story is really about the fact that because my hair never came back, people were looking at me differently. I look at me differently.

Anne

In her early 40s, Anne explores how body size, weight management, athleticism, eating disorders, plastic surgery, tattooing, sexuality, and motherhood have all been elements of transformation in her life. She says,

> Talking about all of these things is so complicated. Like, I never bring it up when I see people's bodies have changed. I wait for the other person

to bring it up. Right? Because I'm not going to bring it up. They say, 'I lost this weight.' That's great. Amazing. 'You must feel great'. Because I don't want to be the one to say something insensitive like people have done with me. It could end with 'Oh, shit. Sorry. You're dying, actually? Great. Well, sorry, you look amazing, though! Like, fuck off.

Ari

Ari's pronouns are they/them. They identify as a researcher, writer, musician, and animal lover. Ari's transformation story explores their identities, advocacy, and art. They articulate how they have dedicated their life to advancing social justice and feminism, anti-racism, and trans rights. Ari encourages you to learn more about them at www.genderqueerme.com.

Audrey

In her mid-60s, Audrey tells a story about strength. She says,

> *I compete for strength. I've competed to be the fittest woman in the world. I succeed in CrossFit games, Team Canada triathlons, I've competed internationally for triathlon. I could go on. This is who I am. I train every day. For my age, I think that my strength and endurance is pretty cool.*

Haz

In their early 40s, Haz (she/her and he/him) is working at a preschool in Kansas, USA. You will notice that I will interchange Haz's pronouns throughout this book to respect all of their pronouns. She describes her relationship to transformation in terms of queerness, name changes, body changes, pronoun changes, and generally embracing changes as life happens. He says,

> *When I was young, I was a young thin girl, and now I'm a young adult who is genderfluid. A man, essentially, yes. And those things are very different. Right? For sure. And my pronouns are he/him or she/her. I'm good either way. And with the journey of my physical body, with its size, at least, it's been interesting.*

Hila

As a social sciences professor, Hila has often considered bodies in relation to the world that they exist within. Hila's story started as one focused on an eating disorder and its intersections with **white privilege,** but then, as our conversation continued, her experiences of fertility treatments and the gendered experiences of fertility were clearly transformational for her.

Jasmine

In her mid-40s, Jasmine is living in western Canada. Her story explores her relationships with fatness, thinness, strength, and emotions. She recounts her experiences of bodybuilding, an eating disorder, mental illness, joy, self-expression, and the perpetual role of transformation in her life.

Jules

As an Indigenous Indian drag queen, Jules has considered their identities throughout their whole life. Jules's pronouns are she/he/they, so I also interchange them throughout this book. She says,

> I saw your call for participants and I felt like I just had to share my story with you. It's not every day that people desire to hear about what it is like to always feel displaced, to feel like who you are isn't quite right, and to have others want to hear about the shifts and changes you have gone through along the way. I'm in my late 30s, but sometimes I feel like I am just getting a grip on the complexity of it all. My brownness, my size, my performance, my desires, my nations – all of it.

Laura

In their early 30s, Laura, who grew up in Europe but now lives in the United States, identifies as a trans hiker. Laura says,

> I started to transition about five years ago. I have had some surgeries that were specifically for my gender presentation or things that were important for me. There are still things that I am changing, but I think that it started not so much with medical transition for me but just self-acceptance, which led to a change in my lifestyle – the hiking – which then led me to go from 220 pounds down to like 160. So, my active transitioning has just led me to finding a belonging in my own body that led to me taking better care of my body and feeling more comfortable and moving more and taking ownership over it again, which led to just healthier life choices. And then obviously, over the last five years, I've gone from being perceived as an average height, random cis dude to a tall woman who is also very athletic.

12 Transforming Bodies

Maria

Maria is a PhD student in English who identifies as a 30-something, queer, **AFAB**, mixed-race person living in Utah in the United States. She says,

> *I consider myself to have two forms of body modification. One, is that I've had top surgery. So, I get misgendered on the street all the time, or people just asking, 'What is that about?' People feel they have the right to approach me. . . . The second is that I have tattoos. I have a half sleeve, full sleeve, I have one leg extensively covered. People approach me about those in the summer, but it is always super-positive. I like thinking about these two aspects of me. Thinking about autonomy and expression, gender presentation, etc.*

Michelle

Michelle is in her late 20s and lives in Canada. Her story revolves around her relationship to disability, specifically her experience with diabetes. She says,

> *There is a lot of just frustration with your body; not understanding what it is doing. There's a lot of times when I was a kid where I would just break down and get frustrated with how my body was behaving. Because there's a lot of need to plan ahead of time, which I believe is a core point as to why I'm not very much of a go-with-the-flow kind of person.*

Ra'anaa

In their late 20s, Ra'anaa has much to say about the experience of change. Crafting a new name, prioritizing art and activism in the Black Lives Matter movement, working on a PhD, using they/them pronouns, and exploring the intersections of Blackness, sexuality, and gender, Ra'anaa is the embodiment of empowerment and transition. They say,

> *I feel great. I feel empowered. And I'm really excited. I really hope that some people are upset by the things I say or do. That is the goal. I hope somebody is upset by, I don't know, what my t-shirt says or the way I'm carrying myself and then they will question to themselves, 'Why are they doing that? Those questions are the goal.*

Rachel

Rachel's story revolves around her identity as an athlete. She tells the story of a time before an injury to her body and all the time that has come after. In her late 20s, Rachel is a marketing advisor in eastern Canada. Her story of transformation is fraught with ambiguity in terms of how she feels reflecting on the changes she has experienced. She says,

> *I played university basketball for five years, but I was an athlete since I was probably four years old. Like, sports was kind of my thing. I didn't do dance or art classes or anything like that. It was just sports. And I loved it. I still do. And basketball in particular has been a big part of my identity, I suppose. So, in my first game at nationals in my final year, 19 seconds into the game, I tore my ACL and everything changed.*

The Author

Since this is a book focusing on storytelling, I figured I should tell you a bit of my story. My name is Victoria (she/her) and I identify as a tall white cisgender settler feminist who is passionate about thinking through bodies and how people understand and treat them. I am a mom, partner, sociology and gender studies professor, researcher, and writer in Ontario, Canada. My interest in bodies was sparked through my years of public scrutiny about my very tall (6′3″) woman's body. The 'scrutiny' I receive is usually from well-meaning strangers who want to talk about my height, but these interactions are never without meaning, innuendo, and feelings. I wrote about these kinds of encounters in my first book, *Gendered Bodies and Public Scrutiny: Women's Stories of Staring, Strangers, and Fierce Resistance* (2021), where I interviewed women about their extraordinary bodies as well as their experiences with strangers commenting on their bodies. It is from the reception that *Gendered Bodies* received that I wanted to keep the conversation going and consider how transformation is another dimension of the ways bodies exist, appear, and are meaningful to us and those around us.

Stories + Art

Interpretation and creativity are key elements of thinking about our bodies and, often, how many of us approach their appearance. As you likely will have noticed, there is some art joining us throughout this book. Part of my intent for this project, which is similar to my last book, is to explore my interest in combining body stories with theory and artistic interpretation. I want

14 Transforming Bodies

to include this artistic element because I think that it is important to recognize how our ways of teaching and learning are often connected to imagery. I asked my artistic collaborator, Damian Mellin, an amazing graphic designer, to work with me again on this new project, but with an entirely different approach. I wanted you to hear directly from Damian about his process, so I interviewed them as well. You will notice that I also interchange Damian's pronouns throughout this book. Damian says,

Who am I? Well, I am a queer-identified man. My pronouns are he/him and they/them. I've always focused on using whatever creative skills that I have to further the social issues that I care about. So, this includes women's rights, as well as the rights of trans and non-binary people. So for me, being able to do something creative to support work like yours is a challenge that I want to take on. You're creating content that tackles deeper issues and sometimes when we tackle deeper issues you need to have something like the art to soften and connect to it differently. I also think for me this project is so interesting, because with my own gender expression – I kind of float right now.

In terms of the imagery in this book, what I focused on is having a representation of the idea of transformation through the images. Because we are working in mostly black and white, I really wanted to focus on how we use tone to convey something. I wanted the animals in these images to be as vibrant as possible, but I wanted the background and the world around these figures to seem a bit almost destitute, like I wanted a very grungy background aesthetic.

For inspiration, I started grabbing ideas from old billboards for women's soaps or super-gendered products from the 1940s and 1950s and kind of scrubbing any of the context off of there. You and I then came up with the idea of showcasing these stories, not from humans, but animal personifications of humans. I know it sounds silly, but crafting these people as people would have been a disservice, number one, because you think of the images as reflections of all of these people, which they are not. Secondly, I wanted an aesthetic that people could get behind because it's cool. I think there is also a freedom for animals to transform and I wanted that to come through. We rarely judge animals. Animals are free to be themselves. I want to create images that actually represent the issues in the book but also images that, like if you saw them, stand on their own. They're really awesome-cool in terms of their patterning, shapes, style, and pose that expressed the topic for each particular piece.

As we work through the book, you will see Damian's art pieces at the beginning of each chapter. The caption for each is expressed through Damian's own words so that you can see how transformation can be discussed in a variety of ways – through stories, art, and theory. I didn't include the full description of Figure 1.1 earlier because I wanted you to have a better sense of the book and Damian's vision before hearing him describe it. Here is a more complete description for Figure 1.1:

> *I chose to use animals to represent transformation because animals have often transformed in stories and we don't really judge them for it. Here, these animals offer us the freedom to give us a bit more of a gender-neutral or gender-non-specific representation, which is so important.*
>
> *To start the book off, I feel like the image needed to be somebody who represents the holding of the keys of these issues. I want somebody who has been through some shit and seen the type of issues we're discussing for a much longer framework. So, I originally had this image of a fox. My thought process was a grandmother who's been around the block, who has supported people in her community. I really wanted that kind of fierce person who embodies the energy of the book. In my design, this is the person who is allowing you to go through the book, who opens the door. This is the person who is inviting you to come in to hear these stories. They are the grandmother figure who is very protective of the stories that you're going to encounter.*
>
> (Damian)

Book Structure

Here are some hints of what is to come in the subsequent chapters and sub-sections of this book.

Chapter 2: Intersections

This chapter focuses on how race, sexuality, and gender intersect and inter-twine. The stories shared in this chapter explore how bodies can be transi-tional spaces. This chapter also explores intersectionality as a theory, with stories that help explain how and why the theory matters to discussions identity.

Chapter 3: Shapes

Chapter 3 introduces body shapes and sizes and how those change over time. A discussion of 'normal bodies,' larger bodies, smaller bodies, and transformed chests are the main subsections. Beyond that, the stories in this chapter also speak to the significance of language, gender affirmation, body positivity, and body neutrality.

16 Transforming Bodies

Chapter 4: Ages and Dis/Abilities

Aging and dis/abilities are transformative experiences. Why pair them together? This chapter explores the ways that the participants connect gender, aging, and their relationship to dis/abilities as significant elements of embodied changes and, at times, embodied challenges.

Chapter 5: Names

Many of the participants have changed their names, not only because of gender transitions but also political activism. This chapter introduces stories of embodied change via the importance of our naming practices and how considerable our names are to how we envision ourselves and connect to other people.

Chapter 6: Performances

This chapter explores the ways that our bodies perform, in terms of how hair, fashion, and tattooing are elements of personal expression and transformation. Considering the theory of gender performativity alongside the role of agency, meaning, and creativity is key to understanding how our bodies perform.

Chapter 7: Bodies Transform

As the final chapter in the book, the focus here is on elements not covered in the previous chapters, namely stories on how to embrace change, live with embodying the in-between, and, finally, advice that the participants offer to readers on the realities of transformation that they have learned. The book concludes with space for you to write your own body story (with prompts to help you craft it), as well as space to be creative – in whatever ways that might mean for you.

At the end of each chapter, you will notice that there is a Key Terms section. The words that appear in this section have been bolded in the chapter and defined in order for your reading to be as accessible as possible. Following the Key Terms section in each chapter, there are Questions for Reflection and Discussion. I hope that these help frame and add to your understanding of each chapter and help you further engage with the ideas you have just read. References and the Index are the last two sections of the book.

Ideally, this book is a tool for teaching and learning. Learning is for everyone, in every place, and the goal of this book is to meet a wide variety of people at various places in your learning journey. The teaching elements found at the end of each chapter are to help you in this.

Key Terms

AFAB – AFAB is an acronym meaning Assigned Female at Birth. AFAB people may or may not identify as female some or all of the time. *AFAB*, as well as DMAB (see next definition), is a useful term for educating about issues that may happen to these bodies without connecting to womanhood or femaleness.

Agender – Agender is a gender identity generally defined as an identity in which someone lacks a gender or has very little experience of a gender. It can be seen either as a non-binary gender identity or as a statement of not having a gender identity at all.

AMAB – AMAB is an acronym meaning assigned male at birth. AMAB people may or may not identify as male some of all of the time. *AMAB* is a useful term for educating about issues that may happen to these bodies without connecting to maleness or masculinity.

Body – The body is a biological, material, and symbolic form of a person.

Body Stories – Body stories are the narratives that we tell about our bodies. These stories can include the physical, social, and emotional experiences and interpretations of our bodies.

Cisgender – Cisgender (often shortened to cis) is a term that refers to anyone whose gender identity aligns with the sex that they were assigned at birth. This identity applies to those people who fully or more closely identify as their assigned sex while simultaneously not identifying with the identity transgender. The word *cisgender* is the opposite of the word *transgender*.

Constructionist Approach – The constructionist approach is a sociological understanding that requires a certain way of thinking about the social world: rather than seeing it as existing separately from you as a person, you have to think about how it is socially constructed or made (and remade) and the implications of different ways of constructing the world.

Embodiment – Embodiment usually refers to how the body is involved in social interactions that create meanings. These meanings are based on how our physical experiences – through bodily form, gaze, gesture, posture, facial expression, and movement – shape the form of our interactions with social and cultural environments.

Embodied Transformation – Embodied transformation refers to the experience of how our bodies transform, as combined with the meanings that those transformations can have – both for ourselves and for others.

Feminist – A feminist is a person who supports or engages in feminism. Feminism is a movement that aims to end **sexism**, sexist exploitation, and oppression.

Gender – Gender refers to the socially constructed roles, behaviors, activities, and attributes that relate to understandings of masculinities, femininities, and non-binary embodiments in every society. Gender is a complex combination of elements that are assigned certain meanings by society, such as an individual's identity, expression, and presentation, as well as the roles and norms associated with those genders. Definitions of gender vary among different cultures and among individuals. Gender is a complex and highly personal experience for all people.

Genderfluid – Genderfluid is a gender identity that refers to a gender that varies and transforms over time. This can be occasionally, every month, every week, every day, or every few moments during a day depending on the person. Sometimes it is consistent and sometimes it is not. A genderfluid person's gender may change dramatically, delicately, rapidly, or slowly, also depending on the person. Genderfluid people may also identify as non-binary or transgender but do not have to.

Genderless – Genderless refers to the experience of not having a gender. A genderless person experiences a complete absence of gender. The term is usually interchangeable with *agender*, but some might prefer it over *agender*, because *genderless* more clearly shows that one does not have a gender.

Non-Binary – Non-binary describes any gender identity that does not fit the male and female binary system.

Privilege – Privilege is a relation of power that positions certain bodies as having unearned advantages that are systemically created and culturally reinforced.

Qualitative Methodology – Qualitative research methodologies seek to capture information that often can't be expressed numerically. These methodologies include some level of interpretation from researchers as they collect information via interpersonal interviews, observation, and so on.

Sexism – Sexism is discrimination based on an individual's attitudes, beliefs, and behaviors, and organizational, institutional, and cultural practices that reflect negative evaluations of individuals based on their gender and/or support unequal status of women and men.

Transgender – Transgender is an umbrella term for anyone whose internal experience of gender does not match the sex they were assigned at birth. Transgender people may experience discomfort or distress due to their gender not aligning with their sex and therefore wish to transition to be the gender they identify with. Transgender people can be any gender. They can have any sexual orientation, express their gender through their appearance in any way, and may or may not fit into society's views of gender. The word *transgender* is the opposite of the word *cisgender*.

Transform – To transform is to have a complete change in the appearance or character of something or someone, especially so that that thing or person is improved.

Questions for Reflection and Discussion

1. What elements from this chapter on embodied transformation are most interesting to you? Where do you think that interest comes from?
2. Does the connection of art and creativity make topics, such as the body or gender, easier to engage in? Why or why not?
3. In the brief introduction to the participants, was there a particular person, or were there particular people, who intrigued you? Whose story, or stories, are you eager to learn more about? Why do you think that is?

References

DeMello, Margo. 2014. *Body Studies: An Introduction*. New York: Routledge.

Kannen, Victoria. 2021. *Gendered Bodies and Public Scrutiny: Women's Stories of Staring, Strangers, and Fierce Resistance*. Toronto: Women's Press.

Orbach, Susie. 2009. *Bodies*. New York: Picador.

Richardson, Niall, and Adam Locks. 2014. *Body Studies: The Basics*. London: Routledge.

Wilson-Raybould, Jody. 2022. *True Reconciliation: How to Be a Force for Change*. Toronto: McClelland & Stewart.

2
INTERSECTIONS

Intersections

FIGURE 2.1 *This image is all about the little intersections. I wanted the signage to be open to interpretation, which is why I've taken away key information. I basically drew out how I'm imagining people moving around on a street and their sexuality, genders, and ages and all of their identities are all up for interpretation. I want the viewer to draw their own conclusions. Having differing gender expressions – cisgender, trans, fluid, fancy, hipster – whatever you see in them, that's okay. Showing intersectionality can be complex because sometimes it's not so easy for some people to be completely open and free to talk about all of their identities, but in this design, they are. Those crossroads can have anything added to them.* (Damian)

Damian Mellin, 2024

DOI: 10.4324/9781003380061-2

My experience of gender transition has been prompted by changes in my attitude and my experiences of my body, but also physical changes, right? And so, I just spend a lot of time thinking and performing and writing and working out my understandings of my body and how it changes and the sort of the potential it has. What I've come to understand in the last several years is that my body is a site of change and can actually be a method for advocacy. And so that's really exciting and inspiring to me.

(Ari)

This is a chapter on intersections. I wanted to start this chapter with a quote from Ari because they beautifully articulate the ways that we can imagine our bodies as transitional places. Ari is referring to their gender transition, but we can also think about transition in terms of what that might mean beyond our physical selves: reflection, social awareness, activism, general thinking, and so on. This chapter explores how our bodies' identities intersect; thinking about intersectionality as a theory and examples to help understand it, as well as discussing race, sexuality, and queerness are the key aims here.

When you think of bodies, you might not imagine intersections or crossroads, but I want to encourage you to think about your body as a site of converging identities. Imagine being in the middle of an empty traffic intersection. The place where you are now exists only because two or more distinct roads have merged or intertwined, thus creating a place that wouldn't have existed otherwise. Or, to think about it another way, imagine taking some paint with a paintbrush. If you add another color to your paintbrush, it is no longer easy, or perhaps even possible, to extract the original paint. Both colors are now changed, intertwined, enmeshed. When we think about who we are, it is also impossible to separate all the elements from one another, especially our identities. Our bodies are not blank surfaces; they have recognizable features, forms, and styles that speak for us to others. These stories are only partial tellings, of course, which is why many people approach bodies that are less recognizable in order to learn more about them. For example, I have often been asked questions from strangers, such as "Why are you so tall?" or, my personal favorite, "Have you always been this tall?"

The role of **identity** is foundational to understanding how bodies appear; it is also a common word that most people use, yet its definition may not be easy to articulate. I consider identity to be a process whereby we relate to others to try to understand ourselves, other people, and groups at any given time in any given place. Identity is not objective or a permanent state, but it changes and transforms over the course of our lives. So, what does this mean? I think that Haz can help explain:

22 Transforming Bodies

I identify as he/him or she/her. Either way, people will ask, "Where do you fall on the gender and identity spectrum"? And early on I was like, "Well, I don't really care either way. But I'm fine being a woman." And then I realized how non-binary that sounds. And I kind of went from there. I was identifying as agender for a while because I saw in others that agender was something I felt connected to. I am very open. With my sexuality and with my gender, I've gone through a lot of different labels. And I find labels useful in that way. I'm not married to them; I don't have to stick with them forever if they don't work for me forever. But I found them very useful in a way of finding community and feeling a part of something and being able to identify this part of myself. And so, I identified as agender and then I kind of kept saying things like, "Man, I wish I was genderfluid. That sounds like fun." And I was like, again, I know that sounds very genderfluid to me, but I don't think that I am genderfluid. And now I would say that I lean more towards male, but I'm not presenting as male at all. I think most of that has to do with the perception that it would take a while before I was perceived as a man and a lot of work. So I'm not even going to try. I'm comfortable. I like wearing dresses. I wear dresses basically every day right now. And I find that comfortable dresses are cute, among other things, in a way that men's clothing never gets quite as cute as a dress. So, I feel like I am a man who likes dresses.

For some people, the ideas that Haz is expressing could be totally new. The idea that you can change your identities based on feelings that you have and that you are not "married" to them means that they can keep changing and that that change is okay. Getting back to thinking about identity then – you might say an identity is something that describes some aspect of who you are – student, friend, or employee. Or you might say something more specific such as cisgender woman, queer, Muslim, middle-class, or disabled. In looking at these identities, it is important to recognize that these categories only exist in relation to the bodies of other people. We identify ourselves by pointing to some element of who we are that we recognize in relation to someone or something else – just as Haz does in her story. While it is true that these identities are constructed (which we will return to soon), that does not mean that they do not have real and tangible effects every single day of our lives.

Ari, who is quoted at the beginning of this chapter, has thoughtfully considered the way that they present their identities and how they characterize these embodied transformations:

And so, I like to think of my experience of transition as some change happens and then we plateau for a while, and then another change happens yet again. You know that there's likely an endpoint. But I did eventually come to find this term genderqueer. For me, it's perfect. So non-binary, as I am not either a man or a woman and while a spectrum is better than a binary, a spectrum still poses masculine and feminine at opposite ends. Right? And so, when I found this term, genderqueer, I was just like, this is perfect, because I'm really explicit about my identity being like a political act. I am choosing to queer gender and that feels comfy and I move through the world intentionally doing that. And so, I really love that word. And my partner, she has been amazing through all of these transitions.

Identities are central to how we understand ourselves, the meanings that we give to our bodies, and they also provide us with a sense of belonging to communities and the people in our lives. As Ari emphasizes, these understandings of ourselves can take a while to coalesce and that "there's likely an endpoint," but the journey to figure out these elements of ourselves is unique to each person. It can take a lot of self-reflection, experience, and compassion to move through the varying understandings that gender offers us.

Identities are also a place where our bodies can experience privilege and **oppression**. The bodies and identities that are seen to be '**normal**' have social privilege. This means that those who are deemed to have 'normal' bodies are afforded social advantages that others are not. As a reminder, privilege can be defined as a process through which certain bodies and identities receive unearned advantages, which are culturally created and reinforced. We can see this in many aspects of life: how women continually earn less money compared to men, how racialized men are more often involved in police shootings than any other people, how employers may see disabled employees as a 'problem' to avoid – someone difficult, someone different, someone who will cost them more to employ.

So, what is normal? A normal body conforms to an average or standard expectation; we can only understand normal in relation to the abnormal – those that are **Other** or different. Of course, the boundary between normal and Other is always precarious and open to change.

I love the idea that shifting happens for everyone. If I look back and think about my eating disorder, the bodybuilding competitions or fitness competitions and to where I am at now, so much shifting has happened. When you transform from being in a quote, unquote fat body to being in a thin body, that transformation is celebrated and praised because everybody's just like "Oh, I can't believe you did that. That's amazing what you did," and then they are talking to you about how wonderful you are. And then when the shift starts to go the other direction – towards a fat body – nobody wants to talk about it anymore.

(Jasmine)

24 Transforming Bodies

Jasmine is reflecting on how her transitions in terms of body size greatly impact how others view her body, discuss her body, and determine various levels of worthiness depending on what size and presentation her body shape is. Sociologist Erving Goffman theorized how our encounters with other people have embodied consequences. In his book *Stigma: Notes on the Management of Spoiled Identity*, Goffman (1963) makes it clear that bodies are inseparable from the meanings and readings that are put upon them by other people. He claims that "[s]ociety establishes the means of categorizing persons and the complement of attributes felt to be ordinary and natural for members of each of these categories. Social settings establish the categories of persons likely to be encountered there" (Goffman 1963, 2). He specifies that these encounters change how we consider ourselves or a stigmatized Other. It is important to recognize that a 'stigmatized Other,' in this instance, is spelled with a capital 'O' (as I did earlier). This is to note the difference between other people – similar to yourself – and Other people – those who have some form of social **stigma**. When we consider what sorts of people have stigmas, then, we can think of all of those who are positioned outside of 'normal' in any given time or place. Throughout history and continuing to today, this list would variously include women and non-binary people, racialized people, Indigenous people, disabled people, queer people, working-class people, older people, and so on.

Intersectionality

> *My identities are complicated. I am part Ojibwe, half Indian and I have brown skin, so people ask me where I am from. I answer that I was born in Canada. That answer is easier for me, more confusing for them. Technically, I am a cis man, but I wear women's clothes to perform. Pronouns are fluid to me. So, people ask me what my gender is. I answer that I am queer. I say that I am everything, but questions follow. I am youthful, so people underestimate me, but I am older than they know and wiser than they suspect. My identities are decidedly intersectional.*
>
> (Jules)

As a person who has continually reflected on their identities, Jules explains the ways that our identities cannot be easily separated. Our identities are intersectional. **Intersectionality** refers to the ways that our identities are never disconnected from each other. When we think about bodies and identities, we need to use an intersectional approach to reflect on how our identities are, well, intersecting. Remember standing at the intersection of the crossroads or the inseparable paint colors from earlier in the chapter? Let's remind ourselves of them now to reflect on intersectionality. Intersectional analyses suggest that biological, social, and cultural categories such as gender, race, class, ability, sexual orientation, and other axes of identity interact and intersect on multiple and often simultaneous levels. These intersections lead to how people experience social privilege and systemic inequality every day of their lives.

Oppressions within society, such as **racism**, sexism, **homophobia**, etc. do not exist independently of one another; instead, these forms of oppression interrelate, creating a system of oppression that reflects the 'intersection' of multiple forms of discrimination. It is also important to remember that these interactions are never outside of relationships based on **power**. More specifically, intersectional analyses suggest that biological, social, and cultural categories such as gender, race, class, ability, sexual orientation, and other forms of identity interact and intersect on multiple and often simultaneous levels.

These relational elements of identity also lead people to experience systemic inequality. The term *intersectionality* was coined by Black feminist scholar Kimberlé Williams Crenshaw in 1989, and has since become pivotal in our understanding of identities. Crenshaw articulated the ways in which Black women's experiences need to be discussed in greater complexity, a formative idea at the time. She states:

> I am suggesting that Black women can experience discrimination in ways that are both similar to and different from those experienced by white women and Black men. Black women sometimes experience discrimination in ways similar to white women's experiences; sometimes they share very similar experiences with Black men. Yet often they experience double-discrimination – the combined effects of practices which discriminate on the basis of race, and on the basis of sex. And sometimes, they experience discrimination as Black women – not the sum of race and sex discrimination, but as Black women.
>
> (Crenshaw 1989, 149)

Crenshaw is saying that the ways that power, identities, and oppressions are always working together and intersecting have enabled how we understand inequities and the complexities of our bodies. When I teach this concept, I tell my students that I can never be thought of as 'just' a woman; rather, I am a white woman with significant social privileges. For example, while I have experienced sexism, I have experienced sexism toward my body through the lens of whiteness and my whiteness must be understood as inseparable from my experience of gender (and all my other identities as well).

Later in this chapter, race, sexuality, and queerness will be the focus, but here, let's discuss intersectionality as a theory to help understand identities and embodied transformations more clearly. Theory can seem intimidating to some people, but we use it to help understand the experiences that we live

26 Transforming Bodies

within. Alane describes her experience of transition as it relates to her breast cancer treatment:

*In one day of my life, the oncology surgeon did a mastectomy and then a plastic surgeon came and did the breast reconstruction. All on the same day, and because I was on the table for so long, I ended up getting a pulmonary embolism. So now I have to be on aspirin for the rest of my life, you know, so that's different too. And also, the surgical oncologist didn't like how some of my lymph nodes looked on this side. And so, he took those out. So, I'm also numb there. My body is so different. I have all these numb parts of my body now. And there are other just weird things, you'd never think of it, but my toes from chemotherapy got really sensitive. It just felt like every round of chemo brought its own gifts with it. I would realize that my mouth is sore this time or my joints are sore this time or whatever. My joints have never quite gotten back to normal. And then after it was all over, they put me on a medication that they wanted me to keep taking. That was an inhibitor, you know, for **estrogen** production because my cancer was estrogen-fed. And that just killed my joints. I could hardly move them. So, my tastes during chemo went away completely and then never came back quite 100%. I have to use a lot of seasoning. A lot of things have changed in my body. But I mean, most of the time, it's fine. I just feel like I have transformed into a different, a different shell than what I had before. But you know, my, my husband's always like, but you're here. I thought I was only 46 years old. But I thought, you know, I don't want to go the rest of my life without breasts, because I felt like that was part of me. And for me, part of being a woman is to have breasts and I also was thinking about my husband and him wanting to have me to have breasts, you know. So, I think for both of us, it was important for that to happen.*

Here, in Alane's story, she is expressing how so many elements of her life have shifted intersectionally through her embodied transformation with breast cancer. Her day-to-day embodied experience includes elements that were not there before, which some would label as disability, but it is also a gendered experience. The gendered elements cannot be extracted from her embodied experience of cancer – they are entwined and enmeshed, one that is unique to Alane. When Amelia discusses her ongoing relationship with breast cancer, it is quite different from Alane's – even though they share a similar prognosis, their relationship to their bodies is entirely their own. Amelia says, "I did not want to put myself through reconstructive surgery, so I just had the one removed, and that was okay. My partner was accepting." In later chapters, you will read more about Amelia's story of gendered transformation through breast cancer, but I include it here to note how intersectional and personal these experiences are.

Breast cancer is gendered in that both Alane and Amelia immediately discuss breast reconstruction as an element of treatment. Of course, there is nothing medically necessary about reconstructing breasts following a **mastectomy**, but there is an expectation that women present their bodies as bodies that have breasts or that they will need to account for why they do not. In both of their stories, they refer to their partners – who are both men – and relate their experience of breasts through a lens of heterosexual relationships. This is not trivial. Breasts are a relation of sexuality as well. The presentation of self, sexual dynamics, and expectations of how bodies should and could look while also experiencing pain, bodily loss, medical treatments, and complications, in addition to the cancer diagnosis itself, is a plethora of elements to juggle at such a challenging time and one that their bodies carry going forward. In Chapter 3, the discussion of chests as an element of gender affirmation is discussed. It is so important to recognize these complexities when we listen to the stories of other people and acknowledge how there are real and embodied social expectations that impact the decisions we make at these times.

Race

> *People look at me like, well, more so white as if I am white. And I'm like, yes, I am. But the thing is, if you are standing next to my grandma, who is Filipino – "pure" Filipina – like, you would think that these two people aren't even related. My dad is Hispanic, and my mom is half Filipino. But I look so white. And it was like, I don't really know how to navigate that. Because, again, raised the way I was, I didn't really have a ton of cultural connections to either of those, my family was very interested in assimilating, raising their kids in a certain way. So, while that is true, you know, mixed race, I'm like, I don't know how much I can or should claim that, you know, in certain spaces, where people have more visible cultural and linguistic kind of connections to their mixed-race identity than I did.*
>
> (Maria)

Race, like gender, is both an identity, an embodied experience, and a social institution. We categorize bodies into various races in order to divide people based on our embodied differences in skin color. However, the physical

28 Transforming Bodies

differences that many people think of as "race" mean very little biologically; however, these embodied differences mean a great deal culturally and socially. "Race is a social, economic, and political system of division and inequality" (DeMello 2014, 101). Inherited physical traits, such as the color of one's skin or the texture of one's hair, have, throughout modern history, become associated with the concept of race. We treat these differences as meaningful because we make them meaningful. Skin color and hair texture are no different from other inherited physical traits – such as height or eye color – and they are far more difficult to distinguish with precision, but throughout modern history, these traits have been given arbitrary social significance, often in order to exclude people determined to be different than what is 'normal.' Vic Satzewich and Nikolaos Liodakis (2013) argue that "race" (which they consistently place in quotation marks to indicate that it is a constructed term) has come to have meaning over time through pseudoscientific classifications, which were used to foster "biologically informed racism" (14). The authors argue that while this was a historical occurrence, racially informed scientific practices continue today in order to attempt to prove that there are significant genetic differences between people of differing racial "origins." Again, these are relations of power. The power to claim certain bodies are somehow less than or Other to privileged, white bodies.

Perhaps a better way to think about these constructions of gender and race is that we, collectively, create them and apply them to how bodies often look or the location of where bodies are. In Jules's story of transformation, he says,

> *I was never given the option to see myself as anything but brown. I'm Indigenous – my mother is part Ojibwe, but my father is from India. So, all people see – in addition to my fabulous outfits – is brown skin. But what is brown? My skin is actually a gorgeous shade of mocha. But what is that? Coffee? And what are you, white? You don't actually look white. You're beige-ish. It's all so ridiculous to try to call ourselves anything. But what I do know is that brown was not what my classmates at a white school wanted from me.*

The limits of language, Satzewich and Liodakis (2013) point out, mean that we use the term *race* to mean a wide variety of things and "despite the analytical problems with the concept of 'race,' Canadian society still tries to measure and quantify 'race' and 'racial diversity'" (20). Jules addresses how these limits of language are ever-present, but we use categories to try to locate how our bodies 'fit' or don't 'fit' alongside other and Other bodies.

The social significance of racial embodiment is made further obvious by the ways that racial identity is managed through the manipulation of laws, politics, citizenship, and the distribution of resources. News media, for example, are frequently complicit in reinforcing biological notions of "race" as unchanging and fixed, thereby shaping public notions of who matters and who is understood as an outsider. Many of these ideas are colonial in origin. In Maria's story earlier, she speaks to her mixed-race identity and how her skin tone, which looks white, often makes her feel like she perhaps can't claim that identity. Minelle Mahtani (2015) argues that people of mixed race are often romanticized as being the embodiment of a post-racial future – an ideal that is often internalized by people of mixed race. Mahtani claims that this superficial celebration of multiraciality is often done without any acknowledgment of the weight and legacy of historical racisms. As a result, a strategic amnesia is taking place – one whereby complex **diasporic** and family histories are being lost while colonial legacies are being reinforced. For Maria, her experience of feeling like her appearance as white precludes her from claiming her racial identity.

Colonization is a lived and ongoing reality around the world. According to Sheila Cote-Meek, "[c]olonization is conceptualized as having four dimensions – it concerns the land, it requires a specific structure of ideology to proceed, it is violent, and it is ongoing" (2014, 18). The role of colonization infiltrates all areas of racial identity. These realities of colonization are complex and speak to how the colonizers' desire for land has led to the dehumanization of Indigenous peoples; the movement and elimination of racialized peoples; violent, forced assimilation; cultural genocide; and the ongoing racist and exclusionary practices that Indigenous peoples have experienced in Canada (where I am from) and around the world for generations. The use of the word *Indigenous* to describe Indigenous peoples is a choice. As Linda Tuhiwai Smith (2012) notes,

> "Indigenous peoples" is a relatively recent term which emerged in the 1970s out of the struggles primarily of the American Indian Movement (AIM), and the Canadian Indian Brotherhood. It is a term that internationalizes the experiences, the issues and the struggles of some of the world's colonized peoples. The final "s" in "peoples" has been argued for quite vigorously by [I]ndigenous activists because of the right of peoples to self-determination. It is also used as a way of recognizing that there are real differences between different [I]ndigenous peoples.
>
> *(7)*

30 Transforming Bodies

Tuhiwai Smith is speaking to the importance of naming practices and importantly asserts that "Indigenous" can also be problematic as it "appears to collectivize many distinct populations whose experiences under imperialism have been vastly different" (6). I have chosen to use "Indigenous peoples" and perspectives in this book in order to speak to the most inclusive usage of the term in Canada while recognizing its potential exclusions.

Earlier, I have used words such as *normal* and *real* in quotation marks to indicate that these are contested ideas. Whiteness is undeniably the privileged race across the world, and it is very important to name it that way. White bodies are often considered to be 'unmarked' bodies. These constructions serve to support the racist notion that whiteness offers "the prestige of being better and superior; it is the promise of being more human, more full, less lacking" (Seshandri-Crooks 2000, 7). Furthering this idea, Ruth Frankenberg and Peggy McIntosh are often credited as creators of a body of feminist theory that has sought to form an ongoing account of the social, political, and cultural advantages afforded to white people in Western society. In particular, Frankenberg's (1993) study of white women enables thinking through whiteness as a site for both the reproduction of racism and challenges to it. Frankenberg claims that whiteness must be understood to be similar to how masculinity is gendered – these aspects of identity are socially constructed and yet have real privileged effects that must be seen as 'interconnected' with other aspects of identity.

Similarly, in McIntosh's (1990) often-cited piece "White Privilege: Unpacking the Invisible Knapsack," she argues that "whites are taught to think of their lives as morally neutral, normative, and average, and also ideal" (32–33). She infers that white people receive social advantages that are conveyed through these notions of neutrality and this neutrality renders the advantages invisible to most white people, but visible to marginalized Others. She also provides a thoughtful warning: "Since racism, sexism, and heterosexism are not the same, the advantages associated with them should not be seen as the same" (McIntosh 1990, 35). While McIntosh doesn't use the language of intersectionality, you can see it underpinning the previous quote and guiding us through a caution of the complexity of identity.

The privilege that I described earlier is often unique to white people, as Ra'anaa says,

It's not like my Black body is ever absent, right? I am always Black. I have always been seen as and treated as Black. The meaning of that for me, though, has changed and is constantly evolving.

How can these discussions of race tie back to embodied transformation? When we can imagine understandings of race as evolving, changing, and manifesting differently throughout the course of our lives, these are embodied transformations. Here, I will use my own example. When I was sitting in my first Women's and Gender Studies course during my undergraduate degree, I remember a moment when I learned that I was white. It sounds ridiculous to me now, but I truly had never considered myself as having a race. I grew up in a rural Canadian city that was predominantly populated by white people. My best friend was Asian, but I had never considered that I was anything other than the norm. My race was not talked about in spaces largely populated by white people. When I left that city and moved to Toronto, a space full of diverse bodies and experiences, my body became clearer to me. In that moment in my class, I was not physically transformed, of course, but my thinking was forever changed by recognizing I was a person in a white body. My relationship with the social world and my understanding of my body as reflecting white privilege were transformative realizations that began to be the filter through which I understood the world around me.

Sexuality and Queerness

> *I came out as queer in 2020 or 2021. And then I started doing a lot of BLM [Black Lives Matter] work, because like all of these activist moments really started to connect me to queer, Black folks. We started doing more queer events, just like talking more about queerness and connecting with a lot of people. And I was like, yeah, yeah, I saw myself in queerness. And just like being around all these people and feeling so much love and attraction for being around all these cool people. And I was like, at the time, I had a partner, and I remember having this full conversation with him and just be like, "I'm queer." And he was like, "Yeah, that's okay." And I was like, wow, this is not the reaction I was expecting from anyone. For some reason. I thought everyone was gonna, like, lose their shit, but they didn't. It just made sense that this is who I am.*

(Ra'anaa)

In Ra'anaa's story, you can see how their identity as queer does not exist outside of their identity as Black. The intersections of identities are crucial to understand here as we cannot, nor should not, try to separate the elements of who we are. As Crenshaw (2020) says,

> What intersectionality is, is a prism, it's a framework, it's a template for seeing and telling different kinds of stories about what happens in our workplaces, what happens in society, and to whom it happens. Now some part on why we are not done, is predicated on what we haven't been able to see, what's not remembered, the stories that are not told. So, intersectionality is like a training wheel to get us to where we need to go. It's glasses, high index glasses, to help us see the things we need to see.

In order to see these intersections, we need to have a better understanding of the meanings of the identities that we have. Feona Attwood (2018) defines **sexuality** as referring to "all erotically significant aspects of social life and social being – desires, practices, relationships and identities, as well as sexual interests, acts, expressions and/or experiences" (6). Sexuality intersects with race and gender in inextricable ways. DeMello (2014) says that "everything related to **sex** – and by that, we refer to your biological sex, the sexual relations that you may have, and your sexual identity and orientation – is shaped by, and understood through, the lens of culture" (137). Our everyday socialization involves exposure to social definitions that distinguish the sexual from the nonsexual, label some forms of sexuality as acceptable and others abhorrent, and construct sexual scripts for masculinities and femininities. These 'rules' are usually conveyed through our language, but they are also conveyed through social behaviors, such as staring or intrusive questions.

Identities are central to our sense of self and can (but do not always) provide us with a sense of belonging to communities and the people in our lives. For example, I have used the acronym **2SLGBTQIA+** and the identity queer. These terms of identity are in need of definition because they can be so fluid in their meaning. For example, 2SLGBTQIA+ includes, but is not limited to, Two-Spirit, lesbian, gay, bisexual, transgender, queer, intersex, agender, asexual, androgynous, genderfluid, and questioning people. **Queer** is an umbrella term in order to ensure that identities of sexuality are as open-ended and inclusive as possible. Queerness is an identity that is both an orientation, a cultural identity, and a community for many of those who identify as 2SLGBTQIA+.

Sexuality is an often misunderstood – or variously understood – term. The role of sexuality in our lives reflects one of the major axes through which we understand ourselves and others. Sexuality, as a core identity for each of us, is a social power dynamic where people can be oppressed, liberated, or exist somewhere in between.

Haz is the perfect example of a person who is always in the process of thinking and rethinking identity:

I was always considering who I was. And so, I struggled with figuring out who I was, while I also didn't want to take up space that didn't belong to me or where I didn't belong. And it's like, it's like, I have friends who do this with sexuality. They're like, I don't know, like, I'm kind of attracted to all genders, but like, I don't know that I'm queer enough to take up space in the community. And I kind of use that as a road map, because anytime anyone said that to me, I was always like, No, it's okay. Right? If you want to identify and take up space in the queer community, you are welcome to it. You don't have to constantly update your bio or your body or anything like that. You can just be a member!

While the role of claiming an identity can definitely be contentious – here we can think of those who claim an Indigenous ancestry and identity to potentially exploit, gain access, and community alongside Indigenous peoples that they have no historical connection to (see Taylor and Kemp 2022). But there are some identities, such as queerness, that are open to be used to speak to the experiences of those who feel outside of the norm, as Haz says above. Sexuality and queerness, much like race and gender, intersect in every story you will read in this book. Sometimes, the focus of a story is on one element of an identity and that is okay, but it is important to remember that all the identities are there and working together to create each person.

In the next chapter, you will read stories from the participants who discuss body sizes and the impacts that their shape transformations have had on their lives.

Key Terms

2SLGBTQIA+ – 2SLGBTQIA+ is an acronym for those who are a part of the queer community. The acronym stands for, but is not limited to, Two-Spirit, lesbian, gay, bisexual, transgender, queer, questioning, intersex, asexual, agender, androgynous, genderfluid, genderqueer, bigender, pansexual, and so on.

Colonization – The large-scale process of colonization involves invading nations, assuming control of Indigenous territory, and applying external systems of law, government, and religion as a process of assimilation and/or genocide of the Indigenous peoples. For example, the Canadian nation was created through a process of colonization.

Diaspora/diasporic – Diaspora refers to a large group of people who share a cultural and regional origin but are living away from their traditional homeland. Diasporic populations reflect instances of mass migration or forced relocation and these peoples are often outnumbered in their new nation of residence.

Estrogen – Estrogen is one of the sex hormones commonly associated with people assigned female at birth (AFAB), including cisgender women, transgender, men and nonbinary people with vaginas. The development of secondary sex characteristics (breasts, hips, etc.), menstruation, pregnancy and, menopause are all possible, in part, because of estrogen (Cleveland Clinic 2024).

Homophobia – Homophobia is the fear, hatred, discomfort with, or mistrust of people who identify as 2SLGBTQIA+.

Identity – Identity is a relational process through which we understand ourselves, others, and groups at any given time, in any given place. Identities include our gender, race, class, ability, sexuality, religion, nation, and other aspects of our personal relationships with one another.

Intersectionality – Intersectionality is a theory that refers to how biological, social, and cultural categories such as gender, race, class, ability, sexual orientation, and other axes of identity interact and intersect on multiple and often simultaneous levels.

Mastectomy – A mastectomy is a surgical procedure to remove breast tissue.

Normal – Normal is a relation where someone or something is deemed to be conforming to a standard that is 'typical' or 'expected.'

Other – The Other is a term used to define another person or people as separate from oneself.

Oppression – Oppression happens when systemic forces limit the opportunities of people who are caught within them. Oppression occurs along socially significant lines, such as gender, race, sexuality, and nation. It is a web of systemic forces that shape the world into its current structures.

Power – Power is used in a variety of ways to mean a relation of social, cultural, economic, material, and physical domination.

Queer – An umbrella term, queer is used to be as open-ended and inclusive as possible. Queerness is both an orientation and a community for those who identify as part of the 2SLGBTQIA+ community.

Race – Race is a socially constructed category that serves to separate people based on practices of exclusion and oppression in relation to ancestry, appearance, and social location.

Racism – Racism involves a racial group having the power to carry out systematic discrimination through social policies and practices and by shaping cultural beliefs and values that support those racist policies and practices.

Sex – *Sex* can refer to the physiological classifications of biological bodies or the practice of engaging in sexual activity and/or intercourse.

Sexuality – Sexuality is a social category that defines our sexual interests, desires, and intimacies. Sexuality has been used as an element of social control to deem some desires as 'normal' and others as 'wrong.'

Stigma – A stigma is a set of negative and unfair beliefs that a society or group of people have about a person, group, or some aspect of society.

Questions for Reflection and Discussion

1. Consider this: Our bodies are not blank surfaces; they have recognizable features, forms, and styles that speak for us to others. What elements of your body do you see as speaking for you?
2. In what spaces or places does your body experience privilege? What does that feel like? How do you navigate it?
3. If you had to make a list of your identities, which ones do you see as most important to you now? Which ones were most important to you five years ago? Ten years ago?

References

Attwood, Feona. 2018. *Sex Media*. Cambridge, MA: Polity.

Cleveland Clinic. 2024. "Estrogen." https://my.clevelandclinic.org/health/body/22353-estrogen.

Cote-Meek, Sheila. 2014. *Colonized Classrooms: Racism, Trauma and Resistance in Post-Secondary Education*. Black Point, NS: Fernwood.

Crenshaw, Kimberlé. 1989. "Demarginalizing the Intersection of Race and Sex: A Black Feminist Critique of Antidiscrimination Doctrine, Feminist Theory and Antiracist Politics." *University of Chicago Legal Forum* 1 (8): 139–67.

———. 2020. "Kimberlé Crenshaw | The 2020 MAKERS Conference – YouTube." Accessed February 4, 2024.

DeMello, Margo. 2014. *Body Studies: An Introduction*. New York: Routledge.

Frankenberg, Ruth. 1993. *White Women, Race Matters: The Social Construction of Whiteness*. Minneapolis, MN: University of Minnesota Press.

Goffman, Erving. 1963. *Stigma: Notes on the Management of Spoiled Identity*. New York: Simon & Schuster.

Mahtani, Minelle. 2015. *Mixed Race Amnesia: Resisting the Romanticization of Multiraciality*. Vancouver: UBC Press.

McIntosh, Peggy. 1990. "White Privilege: Unpacking the Invisible Knapsack." *Independent School*, 31–36. https://precollege-summer.uconn.edu/wp-content/uploads/sites/264/2018/07/McIntosh_WhitePrivilegeKnapsack-19901.pdf.

Satzewich, Vic, and Nikolaos Liodakis. 2013. *"Race" and Ethnicity in Canada*. 3rd ed. Don Mills, ON: Oxford University Press.

Seshandri-Crooks, Kalpana. 2000. *Desiring Whiteness: A Lacanian Analysis of Race*. New York: Routledge.

Taylor, Drew Hayden, and Paul Kemp, dirs. 2022. The Pretendians: The Passionate Eye. Documentary. CBC Gem. *The Pretendians | The Passionate Eye | CBC Gem*.

Tuhiwai Smith, Linda. 2012. *Decolonizing Methodologies: Research and Indigenous Peoples*. 2nd ed. London and New York: Zed Books.

3
SHAPES

Shapes

FIGURE 3.1 *This is my favorite image. I've been so inspired by people who've gone through really big changes in their life. In this case, the orca that we're showing has lost part of their fin, but, that's not the focal point. It's there, but I really wanted the focal point to be that this is somebody outside of people's opinion about their body size, their shape. They're going to the beach. They're gonna have a great time. It's a bit of a messy image and the joy is the focal point, but these other things make them who they are. For me, I've had a number of women in my life who have had double mastectomies and they have these scars. Instead of hiding them, they've kept the scars and they've even tattooed around them. For me, that was the thing to show. This image is one of living in the joy of your experiences and your shape – whatever shape that is.* (Damian)

Damian Mellin, 2024

DOI: 10.4324/9781003380061-3

Shapes **37**

The shape of our bodies change. The texture of them changes. I am not the same person that I was even yesterday. I am more. I add more. I may be physically small, but I am still a large person.

(Jules)

Bodies have shapes. Bodies are shapes. Those shapes transform over the course of our lives. We grow, we shrink. When we discuss our body shapes, though, we rarely use neutral words. Thin. Fat. Huge. Tiny. Tall. Short. As Rosemarie Garland Thomson (2009) says, "Something seems either too big, too small, too much, or not enough as people try to make sense of the seeming incongruity presented by unusually embodied people" (167). These are the words that we use, and they are loaded with meanings. Of course, these are also interpretable words, but mostly we use them to categorize ourselves and other people into somewhat distinct groups or at least groups we determine are appropriate for those words.

I was an overachiever, and I always felt like I didn't quite meet the threshold of a good person, or a popular person, or a well-rounded person, because I wasn't thin. I didn't meet that body ideal that had been set out in all these messages I was getting from magazines and TV shows. I was thinking about getting thin, but I don't think I actually set out to change my weight until I decided to get married, and then the messages just pile on. When you decide you want to get married and you are not a skinny woman, it's like everywhere you turn. To be a worthy bride means you are a skinny bride. So yeah, at that time it was my very first quote unquote, real diet.

(Jasmine)

In Jasmine's story, she describes how her relationship with thinness started to become a pressure point in her life once she planned to get married. The pressure that she felt from **heteronormative** wedding imagery, her idea of what a 'bride' appears to be, and how she envisioned herself in that role led her to begin her first "real" diet, which then also led to a very complicated relationship to her shape:

When I started on the diet program, my body responded really well, and I lost a lot of weight. But it feels like almost being brought into a club of some kind. Like all of a sudden, you belong because you are trying to fit into a mold that you've been assigned with all these messages that you've heard from other people, and people are praising the results that you're getting and you just start to feel that maybe this thinness is obtainable. This is success but it's never enough when you're in the middle of it. I had lost around 80 pounds, and I still looked at myself and thought, you're not thin. You don't look like those people in the magazine.

It was never enough.

So, after the wedding, I was on a fairly normal diet. The first little while, it's okay, but I get hyper-focused, and then thinness becomes the only thing that matters in my life, because the thought process was, if I can just get control of this, I can just get control of my health. If I can just get control of my weight, then I can move on to doing the next goal on my list and put my focus there.

(Jasmine)

Jasmine's discussion of her hyper-focus on the goal of thinness is a common reality that many people can empathize with. Eating disorders, overexercising, and an impossible thin ideal can be preoccupying for people, predominantly women, who receive so many messages that whatever their body is doing, it is not doing the right thing. As Sonya Renee Taylor (2021) argues that

[t]hose of us who believe we do not have the "right body" spend decades of our life and dollars trying to shrink, tuck, and tame ourselves into the right body all the while forfeiting precious space on the planet because we don't feel entitled to it.

(16)

This reality is so important to recognize, and we also need to recognize that a discussion about body shapes must go beyond weight. This chapter focuses on the reality of body shapes – larger bodies + smaller bodies and transformed chests. With the participants in this book, their stories of altering their bodies often surrounded what they call their chests, breasts, and/or boobs.

Breasts are tricky. I have fake ones that I can take on or off for perform- ing [as a drag queen]. But I might get implants someday. I might not. Talking to people about the where, how, what, when, and why of chests is rarely neutral.

(Jules)

Jules is speaking to the complexity of even discussing chests. Switching between *breasts* (often associated with cisgender women's bodies) and the word *chests* in general is part of not only the complexity but also the fact of having them, removing them, desiring them, hating them, and so on. The latter half of the chapter discusses transformed bodies in relation to chests. First, let's continue to break down what a 'normal' body could be.

Normal Bodies

Popular culture often dictates what form and shape our bodies could or should be for them to seem normal and desirable, but that is compounded by the fact that we also live in a time during which most of the images of bodies that we see are filtered, altered, airbrushed, shrunk, made, or augmented by artificial intelligence (AI) and/or have undergone so many manipulations that they can no longer be considered meaningful human representations.

So, what is normal? A normal body conforms to some standard expectation; we can only understand normal in relation to the abnormal, the undesirable, the awe-some, and the odd. As I often teach about bodies in my sociology classes, I always ask students to define what a "normal body" might be (with the caveat that I think this is a problematic question but still a sociologically useful one). When I last asked the question, one student said, "I know that I am whatever normal is," and another student followed this comment up by saying, "I know that whatever normal is, I will never be." Normal is constructed by those who connect with it, desire to connect with it, resist it, and/or feel like they will never connect with it.

Remember in Chapter 2, the idea of stigma was introduced. Goffman argues that bodies are inseparable from the meanings that are put upon them by other people. He is saying that these encounters we have with others change how we consider ourselves and help us determine what kinds of people are normal, and what kinds of people are Other, such as those that have stigma. He says that stigma can

> be used to refer to an attribute that is deeply discrediting, but it should be seen that a language of relationships, not attributes, is really needed. An attribute that stigmatizes one type of possessor can confirm the usualness of another, and therefore is neither creditable nor discreditable as a thing in itself.
>
> *(Goffman 1963, 3)*

Goffman says that the Other's appearance – whatever form of appearance that may be – creates a boundary between what is normal to us and how some bodies "don't fit" with that idea of normal. To further this point, Goffman (1963) brutally says that "[b]y definition, of course, we believe the person with a stigma is not quite human" (5). When we consider what sorts of people don't get to be normal, then, we can think of all those bodies and shapes of bodies who are positioned outside normal in any given time or

40 Transforming Bodies

place. Throughout history and continuing to today, this list would variously include women and non-binary people, racialized people, Indigenous peoples, disabled people, queer people, working-class people, older people, fat people, and this list can go on.

Larger Bodies + Smaller Bodies

Body sizes are seemingly both subjective and objective. There is no wrong way to have a body. Yet there are measurements, medical diagnoses, scales, categories, percentages, and so on that all try to quantify what our body is in relation to some measure of normal. I have never had a normal-sized body. I always joke that I am never even considered an option in relation to any sort of height scale or prediction anyone has ever tried to put me on. A woman who is 6'3" without shoes on is not considered normal in any form of measurement. I have a larger body, but I have also been considered thin. So I have a smaller body, but I am substantially heavier than a 'normal' thin woman, so I have a larger body? Once again, the limits of our language around these markers should demonstrate their uselessness in accurately representing who and what we are.

Hila's story of her body transformation captures this complexity:

> *I was in this bigger body that was starting to get smaller. And so maybe I had lost 20 pounds in the course of a year. But then I went away and did my master's for two years. And I started my PhD, but over the course of my master's degree, my kind of so-called innocent dieting actually was eating disorder behavior. And when you do those behaviors in a larger body, everybody congratulates you, right? And then your body is small, all of a sudden, and those exact same behaviors are thought of as a problem. And so, my body became much smaller. And, you know, in fact, it was probably about 100 pounds altogether smaller than when I was larger.*
>
> *There are a few issues here, but the key one is that I'm in a feminist program and I am well aware of the problems and my eating disorder is becoming, you know, worse. It's getting in the way of life, right? And I know it's not right, and I know it's a problem. And I don't support it for other people. So even though I was sort of really trapped in the behaviors, there was no way I wanted to impart that on other people. So, when I was teaching fitness classes, I did no body talk with them. I was really intentional about not reproducing this kind of really toxic diet culture. But at the end of the day, I'm teaching a fitness class, which is already framed for people as something that leads to weight loss in particular. And I found it so hard to change the direction of conversation. I ended up having, you know, people wanting*

to tell me about their diet and people wanting to ask me advice. And then all of a sudden, I realize that my small body is provoking people to feel shame around food choices and soda consumption. And so, my presence became this kind of policing of other people's bodies. And to realize that was just so horrible, right? Because I know how those kinds of cultural logics are, and just my sheer presence, the cause of the transformation of my body, was having all these effects on people who I didn't even know very well.

Hila's story offers many insights into how our bodies can speak for us in ways that we may not predict. As Susie Orbach (2009) says, "[w]e are judged physically and our social and economic position has depended on how our bodies are seen and where we are then placed socially and economically" (165). But Hila's discussion forces us to recognize how insidious **fatphobia** is. As Sonya Renee Taylor (2021) says, "[f]atphobia remains one of the most challenging forms of body terrorism to beat back" (106). Fatphobia is a weight-based bias that fosters negative attitudes and stereotypes surrounding and attached to larger bodies that are deemed **fat**. Often, fatphobia manifests as an abnormal and irrational fear of being fat or being around fat people. Fatness is meant to be expressed as something 'normal-sized' people should never desire:

> Fat people are afforded a voice or a face when our bodies change or when we express the grief, regret, guilt, and shame that thin people imagine must come from having bodies like ours. What they do not consider is the crumpling that happens when you see your body, every day, represented as a cautionary tale for someone else.
>
> *(Gordon 2020, 137)*

This, of course, then creates thinness as the ultimate goal of a body's shape, regardless of how health is being defined (this, itself, is quite contentious).

The shame placed on larger bodies can be almost unbearable. As Kate Harding and Marianne Kirby (2009) ask,

> How on earth are you supposed to love your body when you're constantly told it's too fat, too hairy, too wrinkly, too zitty, too musky, too short, too tall, too boyish, too curvy, too sweaty, too unhealthy, too mortal, too human?
>
> *(viiii)*

The impossibility of being in the 'right' body might seem more acutely obvious for those whose bodies have transformed between larger and smaller a number of times over their lives.

42 Transforming Bodies

We can think of pregnant bodies as a prime example of a body that is never quite right. In 2013, I published a paper called "Pregnant, Privileged and PhDing: Exploring Embodiments in Qualitative Research" in the *Journal of Gender Studies* (Kannen 2013). When I was working on my PhD, I became pregnant and the impact that my pregnant body had on my research was both unexpected and impossible to ignore, so much so that I felt it had to become part of the results of my study. My pregnant body inspired odd assumptions that became overwhelming at times. This is a common experience for pregnant people because their body is undergoing an obvious transformation that is novel to some people, strange to others, and fairly fast in its pace of change. While the shape and size of pregnant bodies were not a main focus of anyone's stories, we do return to a discussion of pregnancy and transformation in Chapter 7. Whatever form transformation takes in terms of shape, it impacts how we feel.

The emotional element of changing body sizes is key to explore. Anne, for example, talks about how her transformation impacted her mental health, and how it still impacts her relationship with the idea of fatness:

> *The transformation I will never forget was from going from athlete to a larger woman. And I will also never forget when I saw my high school sweetheart walk into where I was working. And he saw me at this and the shock in his face. It just crushed me and then I'm sitting here thinking, I never want anybody to see me anymore. At that point. I don't want anybody from my past to see me. That's because I was always an athletic kid.*
>
> *My mindset now is much better. As long as you're happy and healthy. I'm very comfortable with my body now. But I still have feelings and I'm not going to use the word because I hate the word. I hate it. Like, I can remember somebody saying it to me once they remember what I used to be. I was so hurt. It felt so mean. I feel like whispering it like a bad word. But that was still me and I know it's not a bad word, but there is so much trauma connected to that word for me.*

You should notice in Anne's story that she does not use the word *fat*. When she says, "*I'm not going to use the word*," I asked her if the word was *fat* and she said, "*Yes.*" The avoidance of the word *fat* is because it carries negative connotations with it that are intended to shame fat bodies as though they are undesirable and carry social stigma.

> Thin people especially struggle to say "fat," the hypothetical that has hurt them so deeply. But as an undeniably fat person, the word isn't hurtful to

me. It cannot be, because I do not have the luxury of escaping it. Instead, I am beholden to someone else's discomfort with a word that has never accurately described them.

(Gordon 2020, 159)

For Anne's experience, she does discuss being in a much larger body, but the word *fat* resonates for her as a 'dirty' or shameful word, one that she doesn't want to say aloud. This can be seen as an internalized experience of fatphobia where there is deeply connected shame to an identity that Anne has transformed away from. Again, it is important to recognize that a person's journey is unique, challenging, and always in process.

Laura also describes significant changes in terms of gender transition and altering body shapes from larger to smaller:

I think I started transitioning about five years ago. I have had some surgeries that were specifically for my gender presentation or things that were important for me. There's still things that I am changing, but I have improved radically. I think that it started not so much with medical transition for me but just self-acceptance led to a change in my lifestyle, which led me to go from 220 pounds down to like 160 pounds. So just me finding a belonging in my own body then led to me taking better care of my body and feeling more comfortable. I began moving more and taking ownership over my body again, which led to just healthier life choices and led to my commitment to hiking.

(Laura)

Ambivalence, shame, contradiction, and empowerment can all be wrapped up in the same body story. Our feelings about our bodies do not have to be perfectly woke or perfectly expressed. Anne's story is winding, much like everyone's. The society in which we live dictates so much of how we are meant to feel about ourselves and those around us. Smaller bodies have thin privilege; this is undeniable, but the complexities of size do not simply rest with concepts of large and small.

Body Positivity

Because fatphobia has been prevalent for so long, the body positivity movement could seem like a liberating alternative to the stereotypes of weight-based discrimination. **Body positivity** is a social movement and ideology that promotes a positive view of all bodies, regardless of size, shape, skin tone, gender, and physical abilities. Being able to claim that you love

44 Transforming Bodies

your body's shape, for many, is decidedly an empowering experience. Haz describes the body positivity journey that he went on:

> *When I was about 28, my body started just getting bigger. And I had kind of already worked through what that might be like. I started learning about body positivity, fat liberation, and fat positivity and all of that kind of stuff. Before I became bigger, so I was pretty ready for it. When it did happen, it was like, "Oh, okay, your body's getting bigger. Maybe it's because you're eating a little bit better. Maybe it's just because your body is just changing. And either way, that's okay". And so, I had an interesting experience, where the eating disorder was one thing, and then learning that acceptance of my larger body was another, and then actually becoming bigger was another element.*

Haz is discussing why loving your bigger body is expected to be a journey. Much like we live in a society where straight people do not need to 'come out' as straight, we are expected to mentally prepare for how to handle our bodies becoming larger. In Aubrey Gordon's (2020) book *What We Don't Talk About When We Talk About Fat*, she claims that

> [b]ody positivity has widened the circle of acceptable bodies, yes, but it still leaves so many of us by the wayside. Its rallying cry, love your body, presumes that our greatest challenges are internal, a poisoned kind of thought about our own bodies. It cannot adapt to those of us who love our bodies, but whose bodies are rejected by those around us, used as grounds for ejecting us from employment, healthcare, and other areas of life.
>
> *(158–9)*

Gordon is addressing how body positivity must come from within individual people and is not really changing any sizeist assumptions about fat bodies. She goes on to argue that discrimination against larger bodies and fatness, in particular, will only be successful when all bodies are actually acknowledged. Gordon claims that clothing lines and other advertisements that celebrate "all bodies" are primarily only making visual the bodies that are considered idealized representations: "The most recognized faces of body positivity, frequently models and actors, are disproportionately white or light-skinned, able-bodied, and either straight size (that is, not plus size) or at the smallest end of plus size" (6). This debate about size representation was clear in Jasmine's story of her fat identity as well.

Jasmine connects with the word *fat* but simultaneously reflects on what it might mean for her to be part of the fat community:

I think fat is a descriptor for me that I like, but I know that's not how our culture sees it. I completely recognize that it's meant to be derogatory. But there is something really empowering about being okay with the word, because if someone comes at me with some type of stupid comment like, "You're just a fat, whatever", it is something powerful and being able to reclaim that, you know? So, I've gotten very comfortable with that word, but that has taken years because so much of my story was wrapped up in this idea of avoiding being fat at all costs.

I feel like we live in a culture where anyone can recognize themselves as being part of a body-positive community and as part of a body liberation community. But I also think that no matter who you are within that community, you need to recognize privilege, because if you are like me, I'm what is considered a small fat, rather than superfat. The difference is significant, so, for me, the reality is that in most cases people don't openly gawk at me on the street. I don't have a problem sitting in spaces with arms on the chairs. I don't need a scooter to get around. I can buy clothes in most plus-size clothing stores and those stores exist in the city that I live in. I can even sometimes find stuff in straight size clothing stores depending on how big the cut is. And those are big deals, because if you don't have access to those kinds of opportunities, life can be made challenging. I've heard so many horror stories, like a stranger pulling things out of your own grocery cart because they think you are too fat, as an example.

Jasmine's story positions her feelings about the privilege that her body affords her based on the size of her body. In terms of this, she also introduces a few key ideas: small fat and superfat. Phrasing such as "superfat, "mid fat," and "small fat" are meant to be used as identity markers for those in the fat community. Gordon (2020) claims that

liberation must explicitly name fatness as its battleground – because when we don't, each of us are likely to fall back on our deep-seated, faulty cultural beliefs about fatness and fat people, claiming to stand for "all bodies" while we implicitly and explicitly exclude the fattest among us.

(6)

Charlotte Zoller (2021) adds that the language used to characterize the fat community is intended to be mindful of inclusion while recognizing the variations of fatness that exist:

These are designations on the spectrum of fatness, a set of terms created by and for the fat community to self-identify one's size. These size categories

46 Transforming Bodies

aren't universally agreed upon – folks can identify however they please – but serve as a general outline for where one falls on the spectrum of fat privilege. Those who fall on the smaller end of the size spectrum are afforded more privileges than those on the opposite end. The further you go on the larger side of the spectrum, the more likely a person is to face discrimination, institutional sizeism, be denied medical care, face trouble accessing public spaces, and more. Within the fat community, these designations allow for a shorthand when sharing information. For instance, if I'm in need of a new pair of jeans, I can ask a Facebook group, "I'm a mid fat looking for some new wide leg jeans. Any suggestions?" That way, those who respond know what general category of store I would be able to fit in.

These markers of identity are not perfect. Zoller acknowledges that these categories are not as inclusive of men, trans, and non-binary folks as it could to be, but the list Zoller provides: Inbetweenie or Mid Size, Small Fat, Mid Fat, Lane Bryant Fat, Superfat, Infinifat, and Death Fat are used to give language and categories (sometimes cheekily) to the variety of fat bodies that exist. While the actual sizes might relate to clothing, such as a small fat being anywhere from a size 14 to 18, the reality is that sizing and measurement is not the point; rather, the ability to claim these identities can be radically meaningful in a world that aims to deny their existence.

Transformed Chests

Stories of shapes also relate to transformed chests. **Top surgery**, chest masculinization, mastectomy, double mastectomy, breast reduction, and breast augmentation are all terms used by the participants who have transformed their chests. Ari and Maria both have had top surgery as a practice of **gender affirmation**. Top surgery is a procedure that removes or augments breast tissue and reshapes the chest to create a more masculine, feminine, or neutral appearance for transgender and non-binary people. Gender-affirming care, as defined by the World Health Organization (WHO 2024), encompasses a range of social, psychological, behavioral, and medical interventions designed to support and affirm an individual's gender identity when it conflicts with the gender they were assigned at birth (**gender dysphoria**). Maria describes her decision for this procedure in terms of how it helped her navigate her experience of dysphoria:

I had top surgery about six years ago. Now, the way I describe my identity is butch chick. I had pretty severe dysphoria. You know, prior to that, I had a pretty large cup size. And it just didn't. . . . That part of my body did not fit with my perception of myself. But it was a struggle to articulate that for a very long time because I had this perception in my head of who I was, but it was in my mind only. I was also raised by very Catholic parents and they don't do transgressive gender things. Second of all, even when I went to college and started learning about top surgery, the perception that I received was that this is for trans rights, right? And so, I was like, am I a trans guy? I don't think so. But I'm doing the whole binding thing. I'm looking into this surgery, etc. It became a gradual realization that I can do it for whatever reason. It was entirely for gender affirmation.

Maria's story of a chest transformed is not a usual one. Usually, a story of top surgery is told in strict relation to a transgender affirmation story, but Maria's story points to the complexity of presuming that how we look must decidedly connect to a normative understanding of gender. It does not.

Ari's story of top surgery, while perhaps more expected in relation to a trans narrative, has its own unique priorities: the ability to sing.

I started to feel uncomfortable with my breasts. And so, I started doing a lot of reading of blogs and vlogs. The online community is a great resource in many ways for trans folks. And, in addition to the Discovery Channel documentaries, there's just a plethora of experiences you can learn from online. And so, I was reading a lot about binding and it was sort of like a gradual process that I realized that I'm not sure I really liked my boobs. And that was really the most embodied discomfort I had with them and they were like a B cup – they weren't very big. So, I was actually able to bind relatively successfully, if you will, like I know a lot of folks who have bigger chests and have a hard time doing that. And at the time, I was in my early 30s, so I could afford a binder. I didn't have to ask my mom to buy me one kind of thing. I had that freedom. And, so I was doing that, but it's not comfortable and I've sung for my entire life. Most of my life has been in choirs. But the binder can get in the way of breathing. Right? My singing is incredibly important to who I am, so I started the process to consider what my top surgery might look like, what are the options, all that kind of stuff. And that was very arduous and while Alberta Health covers top surgery, there's a grand total of two psychiatrists in the province who can qualify you for that. And then at the time, I think it was three surgeons and so I got on those waitlists. But, at this point I was almost 40. I did so much research. It's an exhausting process. Luckily, I had the resources and I have a credit card. So, I did it and it felt great. Of course, there was surgery and recovery, but it was fine.

(Ari)

48 Transforming Bodies

In their interviews, both Ari and Maria discuss the complexity involved in trying to navigate the medical system while also reflecting on how hard it is for youth who want this basic care as well. Haz, who has not had top surgery but discussed it in his story as something they might desire in the future, noted,

> And then with being trans, it's interesting. I haven't made any physical changes to my body even though I would like to. I also don't necessarily want to do it in the order that people expect me to. Because I want to get top surgery, but I don't really want to be on **testosterone**. HRT (**hormone replacement therapy**) isn't for me, right now. Which is not unheard of, because then there are major financial questions. How much would it cost me? What hoops am I gonna have to jump through to get there? It is a lot of hoops. It might take years.

Recently, there are cultural debates about the ability for gender-nonconforming youth to access gender-affirming care, and, even though all the stories presented earlier are from people well into adulthood, their experiences of research, medicalization, psychological assessment, and so on is still laborious and mentally taxing. As a non-trans person, Maria said,

> I fudged my own personal story to the mental health provider who gave me the letter of permission. In the area of Ohio where we lived, you had to get the letter saying that this person is mentally sound and they have a reason for a gender-affirming surgery. And so, I had kind of gone into that being like, I have to make my case as a trans guy. It worked. I haven't regretted it. I don't think there was any other way.

While Maria claimed the identity of trans to access top surgery, there is an interesting contrast that occurs in stories of getting **breast augmentation**. Breast augmentation – also known as augmentation mammoplasty – is a surgical procedure aimed at increasing breast size. It involves placing breast implants under breast tissue or chest muscles. Breast implants have been an incredibly common procedure that involves no psychological assessment to access, even though it, too, is a gender-affirming practice.

If you recall from Chapter 2, Alane and Audrey tell the stories of how they navigated breast cancer and mastectomy, as well as how they reflect on their decisions to receive breast augmentation (getting surgical breast implants) or not. These discussions of augmentation are also gender-affirming practices for people. While the definition offered by the WHO earlier notes that gender-affirming care is intended to support and affirm an individual's gender identity when it conflicts with the gender they were assigned at birth, gender affirmation can relate to all genders. Cisgender people are constantly doing things that make them feel better, comfortable, or supported in their gender too. As a cisgender woman, I buy clothes and makeup that make me feel feminine in the ways that I am interested in. These aren't traditionally seen as a form of 'gender affirmation' because unlike trans people, cis people aren't required to affirm their gender for it to be seen as real or valid. However, in Anne's story, it is clear that she received breast augmentation as a practice of gender affirmation:

> I do associate my body with sexuality. Absolutely. I had always been small chested. When I was later on in life, especially after I lost all the weight, I didn't have anything breast-wise. So, I had breast implants done.
>
> Do I love [my breasts]? Absolutely. I love them. I do feel like they fit my body perfectly. I feel more sexual with them and attractive for my husband. He calls them the twins. Ha ha. But, you know, it was for me. It was something that I wanted to do for myself for a very, very long time because I had always been less than an A-cup and they make me feel more like myself.

For Anne to say that she "*didn't have anything breast-wise*" meant that her breasts were not the larger size she desired them to be. She had breasts, but they did not conform to the ideal shape that she had in mind for them. Anne also discussed how she had excess skin removed after she became smaller. These are not unusual transformative practices, but they are gendered ones. As Lindsay Kite and Lexie Kite note (2021),

> [t]hinness is still an imperative – large, firm breasts and smooth, rounded bottoms – are also required. That means many girls and women will go to even greater lengths to achieve a look that rarely occurs in nature by surgically altering their bodies in order to shrink some areas and enlarge others.
>
> (63)

Focusing on transformed chests is an important element of gendered relationships to our bodies and practices of gender affirmation. How we discuss chests, breasts, pecs, tits, boobs, and surfaces, plus how we change them, think about them, and feel about them is all dependent on the meanings that we, and those around us, give or assign to them. Those meanings can also transform for some people and they may never transform for other people.

Body Neutrality

As a conclusion to this chapter, I want to consider the idea of **body neutrality**. Body neutrality prioritizes how our bodies function, and what the body can do, rather than its appearance. As discussed earlier, body positivity can often seem unattainable for those engaged with healing, shame, or doubt in relation to the ways that their bodies have transformed. For some, the role of positivity might seem too much of a leap. "Body neutrality does not negate body positivity – they can work in tandem. But what I do want to explore is how toxic or fake positivity can be just as damaging as body shame" (Meyers 2023, 25). Bethany C. Meyers (2023) argues that we often create new ideals in the face of body positivity in the hopes that we will love our bodies "if": "If only we can get to a certain weight or [if we] fit into a certain pair of jeans, then we will finally be at peace with our body. But that rarely happens" (19–20). Hila also speaks to body neutrality, which we return to in Chapter 7. Hila says,

> There actually are ways to learn to at least be body-neutral. Obviously, you don't have to love your body but you don't have to hate it. I think that's a really worthwhile project to do as soon as humanly possible because, letting yourself be consumed by body preoccupation is not time well spent.

Recognizing our bodies for what they are, in this moment, right now and being at peace with them might be a major challenge for you or those around you, but like everything else with our bodies, there is room for change.

Key Terms

Body Neutrality – Body neutrality is the act of taking a neutral stance toward your body – both emotionally and physically. It refers to not supporting negative feelings towards a body's 'limitations' while also not investing time and energy to love it.

Body Positivity – Body positivity is a social movement that promotes a positive view of all bodies, regardless of size, shape, skin tone, gender, and physical abilities.

Breast Augmentation – Breast augmentation is a surgical procedure that involves using breast implants or fat transfer to increase the size of your breasts.

Fat – The meanings of fat bodies are socially constructed and change over time. In the Industrial period, men who were fat could be seen as representing wealth and power. Fat could be beautiful for women as sign of their husband's wealth, but it could also symbolize greed. Fat bodies, much more recently, represented a lack of control over one's desires, poor nutrition, and laziness. Rather than using medical terms like *obese* or *overweight*, fat activists have reclaimed the identity and treat the word *fat* and/or *Fat* as a valid and celebrated part of their self-identity, granting neutral and/or positive connotations to it.

Fatphobia – Weight bias, also called fatphobia or weight stigma, describes the negative attitudes and stereotypes surrounding and attached to larger bodies. Furthermore, fatphobia is an abnormal and irrational fear of being fat or being around fat people.

Gender Affirmation – Gender affirmation is an umbrella term for the range of actions and possibilities involved in living, surviving, and thriving within a gendered body. While traditionally used to refer to the experience of trans people, gender affirmation are practices that all gendered people participate in. What gender affirmation looks like for every individual person is unique and based on what is personally affirming, what feels safe to do, and what is accessible and available.

Gender Dysphoria – Gender dysphoria is the feeling of discomfort or distress that might occur in people whose gender identity differs from their sex assigned at birth or sex-related physical characteristics. Transgender and gender-diverse people might experience gender dysphoria at some point in their lives.

Heteronormative – To be heteronormative is to hold the assumption that most or all people are heterosexual or straight and cisgender unless stated otherwise; it's about what we consider the default or 'normal' existence of people.

Hormone Replacement Therapy – According to pflag.org (2024), hormone replacement therapy is a type of gender-affirming treatment that allows trans and gender-expansive people to medically transition or feel more at home in their bodies. Those taking testosterone (masculinizing hormones) may grow more facial/body hair and notice their voices deepening. Those taking estrogen (feminizing hormones) may see some breast growth and decreased libido. Many intersex people take HRT to balance the naturally occurring levels of estrogen and testosterone in their bodies. Benefits of such therapy can include improved mental and physical wellness, and reduced anxiety and dysphoria, for those who experience it.

Testosterone – Testosterone is a hormone that sex organs mainly produce. More specifically, the testicles in people assigned male at birth (AMAB) and the ovaries in people assigned female at birth (AFAB) produce testosterone. Levels of testosterone are generally much higher in people AMAB than in people AFAB. Testosterone is used as an element of masculinizing hormone treatments because it stops menstrual cycles and lowers the ovaries' ability to make estrogen (Cleveland Clinic 2024).

Top Surgery – Top surgery is surgery that removes or augments breast tissue and reshapes the nipples and chest to create a more masculine or feminine appearance for transgender and nonbinary people.

Questions for Reflection and Discussion

1. When you reflect on the language used in this chapter to describe differing experiences of bodily shapes, which ones do you see as most positive? Most empowering?
2. Some people dislike when neutral terms of body parts are used, such as how I used *chests* in this chapter. Why do you think they dislike that?
3. If you look at the list of key terms, which word did you learn more about? Is there any other word from this chapter (or the previous ones) that you feel should be on the list because they need more explanation?

References

Cleveland Clinic. 2024. "Testosterone." https://my.clevelandclinic.org/health/articles/24101-testosterone.

Garland Thomson, Rosemarie. 2009. *Staring: How We Look*. New York: Oxford.

Goffman, Erving. 1963. *Stigma: Notes on the Management of Spoiled Identity*. New York: Simon & Schuster.

Gordon, Aubrey. 2020. *What We Don't Talk About When We Talk About Fat*. Boston, MA: Beacon.

Harding, Kate, and Marianne Kirby. 2009. *Lessons from the Fat-O-Sphere: Quit Dieting and Declare a Truce with Your Body*. New York: Perigee.

Kannen, Victoria. 2013. "Pregnant, Privileged and PhDing: Exploring Embodiments in Qualitative Research." *Journal of Gender Studies* 22 (2): 178–91.

Orbach, Susie. 2009. *Bodies*. New York: Picador.

Pflag.org. 2024. "Hormone Replacement Therapy (HRT)." https://pflag.org/glossary/.

Taylor, Sonya Renee. 2021. *The Body is Not an Apology. The Power of Radical Self-Love*. 2nd ed. Oakland, CA: Berrett-Koehler Publishers.

World Health Organization. 2024. "Gender Incongruence and Transgender Health in the ICD." Gender incongruence and transgender health in the ICD (who.int). Accessed February 13, 2024.

Zoller, Charlotte. 2021. "What Terms Like 'Superfat' and 'Small Fat' Mean, and How They Are Used." *Teen Vogue*. Accessed February 13, 2024.

4
AGES AND DIS/ABILITIES

Ages and Dis/Abilities

FIGURE 4.1 *When I approached this chapter on age and dis/abilities, I connected with the idea of health. I really want to make a scene about connectivity. I wanted the vibe to be that these were people of various ages and abilities who knew each other and about to get together. This is just another day. There is a vibrancy to being older, doing activities, and feeling involved in their community. Accessibility is also about showcasing the thing that is special or unique about them. The balcony isn't a barrier; it is allowing them to connect before they move on with their day. These two have amazing fashion, they use supports, like wheelchairs or the cane, to equalize their existence. Fun.* (Damian)

Damian Mellin, 2024

54 Transforming Bodies

> *I am 64 and I've never been stronger in my life. I compete internationally in Crossfit. I get a lot of compliments on how I look and what I do. Last year, I was the second fittest woman in the world for my age group. I have worked out all my life, so activity is just a part of who I am. I get letters from strangers telling me they admire me. And it's kind of humbling in a way. I never quite know how to react. It's pretty cool as you get older for people to admire what you are capable of.*
>
> (Audrey)

> *I don't think I will live that long, as I have chronic conditions that disable me. I feel strong inside and in my [drag] shows, I project that I am strong and young, but it is all an act. Just like drag, I am performing ability.*
>
> (Jules)

This chapter pairs ages and dis/abilities together because these identities are often discussed alongside each other in subtle *and* not-so-subtle ways. In the chapter-opening quotes, both Audrey and Jules refer to their ages as having an impact on what is expected of their bodies in relation to dis/ability. I am putting a slash between dis and ability because as disability studies theorist, Dan Goodley (2018) argues, saying dis/ability emphasizes how much disability and ability rely on one another conceptually. He also uses the slash, not to foster a binary between us (nondisabled) versus them (disabled), but rather, he notes that "[a]bleism and disablism feed off each other; they are co-terminus. This is because disability cannot exist without ability. We would not be able to comprehend disability without its mirror image" (7). To simply use the term *disability* alone ignores the reality of ability and **ableism** that must be paired, so the slash helps to speak to the privilege of ability and make it visible.

Disability, much like gender and race, can be thought of as a representation, a cultural interpretation of bodily difference, and a comparison of bodies that gives structure to social relations and institutions. Scholars in feminist disability studies often explore how bodies labeled as 'abnormal' are treated and excluded from social spaces, as these people/bodies are often used as symbols to represent the 'worst of society' in terms of social ills or deviance. Disability scholars and activists argue that it is in fact *the world* that is built improperly for some bodies and the problems never lie in disabled bodies but in disabling environments (Fritsch 2019). If we think of how some bodies cannot navigate stairs, we can frame the stairs as being the disabling object, not the body that is unable to use them. The stairs are the problem. In this way, we are framing disability in terms of also being socially constructed.

From infancy, bodies are expected to function and behave as 'normal as possible,' and failing to seem 'normal' has social consequences. In *Autobiography of a Face* by Lucy Grealy (1994), she recounts the ways that her life was impacted by Ewing's sarcoma, a potentially terminal cancer that required the removal of a third of her jaw when she was nine. Her reflections on her embodied journey through cancer, pain, and, what she calls, ugliness position the immediacy of her body at all times:

> Often, I tried to balance the pain out with the rest of my body, a sort of negotiation in which I'd isolate one section. I'd lie there and list to myself the parts that didn't hurt, trying to feel them, aware that normally I'd have no reason to "feel" my body or know it so intimately.
>
> I was becoming aware that I was experiencing my body, and the world, differently from other people. For hours I'd lie in bed either at home or in the hospital and run my fingers back and forth along the wall or the bedrails beside me, conversing silently with myself in the third person, rationalizing the situation, setting down the basic premises of my secret philosophy, occasionally even telling myself I was lucky, lucky to have this opportunity to know such things. At times I was desperate and could find no solace anywhere.
>
> *(Grealy 1994, 83)*

The inclusion of this quote is to reflect on how we can hold so many positions at once. Feeling pain and luck, grateful for the experiences and bodies that we have, while also knowing that a "normal body" is one that might be easier to navigate in this ableist world.

Thinking about disability as socially constructed differs from the more common approach to studying disability – as something that needs to be repaired because it is wrong. As discussed earlier, **ability** functions as a stand-in for "normal" – whatever normal is in a particular cultural moment, space, or time defines what ability is. The disabled body/identity acts as a social signifier for deviancy (the abnormal).

> Because disability is defined not as a set of observable, predictable traits like racialized or gendered features – but rather any departure from an unstated physical or functional norm, disability highlights individual differences. In other words, the concept of disability unites a highly marked, heterogeneous group whose only commonality is being considered abnormal.
>
> *(Garland Thomson 1997, 24)*

It is through this loose definition that it becomes clear that disability is socially constructed. The constructed nature of disability is characterized by such factors as expectations of performance; the pace of life; the physical and social organization of social environments to fit a young, nondisabled, "ideally" shaped, healthy adult (male) citizen; cultural representations; failure of representations; visible/invisible representations; and discrimination. The

56 Transforming Bodies

defining of certain bodies as problems, as wrong, and as bad is the oppression that is at the core of the disability rights movement: "Locating the problems of social injustice in the world, rather than in our bodies, has been key to naming oppression" (Clare 2001, 360). We are so often taught to place the onus of problems on the individual, it is challenging to reimagine what it would mean to say that the body isn't the problem.

Connecting these ideas back to age may seem odd, but in the stories of the participants in this chapter, the connections between disability, health, wellness, and bodies all intersect with frameworks of **age**. What do I mean by frameworks of age? Well, age is an identity that is also challenging to define, likely because it seems as though it is the most straightforward identity that we have. A framework of age incorporates stratification – the way that we hierarchically rank people into age groups within a society. These age groups are variable and are used for many purposes to create manufactured boundaries and lump certain people into groups based on a number that has very little to do with the reality of the lives of those in that group. **Age stratification** could also be defined as a system of inequalities that are linked to age. In Western societies, for example, both older and younger people are perceived and treated as relatively incompetent and excluded from many elements of social life, while those in between those two ranges are privileged in that they are seen to embody a desirable age – not too young, not too old.

We Are All Ageist

Theories of aging are often hard to discuss because the complexities of language make them a struggle. For example, the descriptors for age: young, old, senior, elder, child, young adult, middle age, ancient, and so on are all relative terms used to categorize people and place them within certain cohorts. Of course, these cohorts are not consistently assigned, reflect people's actual lived experience, and are all dependent on context. But we still use them to help understand what a certain group of people within a certain age range may experience. You will gather from the stories in this section that these words are all used with varying degrees of meaning.

Ageism refers to the stereotypes (how we think), prejudices (how we feel), and discrimination (how we act) toward others or oneself based on age. In Ashton Applewhite's (2016) book, *This Chair Rocks. A Manifesto Against Ageism*, she argues that ageism "begins as a distaste for others, and in the case of age (as opposed to race or sex), it turns into distaste for oneself" (17). For example, very young children quickly become aware of their cultures' age stereotypes. From three or four years old and onward, they internalize and use these stereotypes to guide their feelings and behavior toward people of different ages (Applewhite 2016). They also draw on each culture's age stereotypes to perceive and understand themselves, which can result in self-directed ageism at any point in our lives. As Applewhite notes, ageism intersects and exacerbates other forms of identity including those related to gender, race, and disability.

These intersections were evident in Amelia's story about what has changed for her body since surviving breast cancer. Her story strongly connects her transformation to her hair and how it has changed her sense of self and what she imagines others think of her:

> *I struggle in Zoom meetings because you just look at yourself . . . because that is not what I used to look like and it is really hard to reconcile it every single time you look in the mirror. You look at a photo and I question "What's my good side?" because either side, I have a huge bald spot. So, I hate photos. I mean, I already hated having my picture taken before my treatment. I was just self-conscious, because I always had body issues. So that's another thing. But now it's even worse. Because now I see . . . because now I feel as old as I look in pictures. Inside, I feel like the person I used to be. It's the reflection that reminds me.*
>
> (Amelia)

Aging is a transformative process that happens simply with the passage of time. In moments, this can seem to be sped up by various experiences that we go through – as Amelia expresses in her story. Transformation doesn't always happen at the interface of age stratifications, because it can happen at any point throughout our aging process. In Applewhite's book, she says the following in relation to aging: "Unless we come to terms with the transition, we hate what we are becoming" (17). I see this as speaking to the ways that ageism is more ingrained than other forms of discrimination, and it is used to discriminate against younger people *and* older people not only on an individual level but also on a wider, structural level. In her earlier comments, Amelia is speaking to the complexity of illness, but also to the pressures of being in a feminine, aging body. As Lindsay Kite and Lexie Kite (2021) say,

> [w]e see women, including ourselves, as bodies first and people second. Boys, men, and people of all gender identities are not immune to the phenomenon of self-objectification, but it is particularly rampant among girls and women or those presenting themselves in a traditionally feminine way. (6)

Body issues, looking "old" in photos, thinking about which side is the good side of our face – these are gendered discussions that intimately connect with the idea that aging is bad for women.

58 Transforming Bodies

Jules also reflects on her relationship with age (which you can see at the start of the chapter) but elaborated to describe this relationship as structural, as well. Jules says,

*Age is just a number, they say. But, that's a lie. Age is a "dirty little" secret we keep to ourselves and try to deny as much as possible. Except for **cishet** men – the George Clooney's of the world don't need to hide their age!*

There is an element of social construction, both local and global, in the way individuals and institutions define who gets to be considered an older person; that is, the shared meaning of the concept of senior, elder, or even 'an old person' is created through interactions among all people in society. This is made clearer by the truism that 'you are only as old as you feel.' The underlying fear of aging, though, is more complex. As Applewhite (2016) says, "[i]t doesn't take much head-scratching to deduce that a tremendous amount of our apprehension about growing old is rooted in fear of becoming disabled" (103). Also key to our discussion, as Jules notes, certain bodies and identities can age more easily, as the expectations of gender and youthful beauty cause femme bodies to go to, at times, extreme lengths to deny any reality of aging.

Ageism exists on a multitude of levels. Ageism against younger adults or children, sometimes termed **youngism** or juvenile ageism, functions mainly as a cohort bias rather than a life-stage bias. This means that despite the young life stage being viewed more favorably than the later life stage, younger adults and children are often assigned unfavorable stereotypes due to their generational differences from older adults. Young people are often presumed to be looking for attention, not telling the truth, exaggerating stories, and so on. The youngest participant in the book, Michelle, who is in her late 20s, speaks to the ways that youth can intertwine with disability to cast doubt on the authenticity of young people when they behave in undesirable ways:

I was seven. It was about seven days after Halloween. It was the crappiest time for a kid to find out they were diabetic when they had candy all this at home. But for a week or so or a little bit before that, I was losing weight and I was getting super tired. I was constantly drinking water; I was constantly going to the bathroom to pee. And my parents were starting to wonder as to what was wrong with me because I wasn't as active as I usually was. And, I was getting cranky. For all of these reasons, my teachers actually started complaining to my parents about me. And they were complaining because I was constantly asking to go to the bathroom and that was disruptive – according to them. And I think I fell asleep in class. And my teacher got really upset at me . . . [long pause] So anyways, finally my dad decided to bring me to the clinic. And at that clinic, they didn't have as sophisticated machines as they did at the hospital. So, when they did the test, the fingerprint tests, they took my blood. And it just said high blood sugar on the machine, but it didn't specify anything. So, he said, "Yeah, you're gonna go to the hospital right now." And they ended up calling ahead of time. They took us in right away. And what my dad told me not too long ago was that the doctors were actually surprised I was still awake. So, my blood sugar was at 46. And for reference it is only supposed to be between four and seven. The doctor was very surprised that I wasn't already in a coma. And I ended up staying there for three to four days with an IV in my hand until they finally got my blood sugar down. And then I got put into a system with the Diabetes Care Center. So, I still go and see them less than 10 times a year, but it depends. From that moment forward, I am taking injections and checking my blood sugar and thinking about this every day. My teachers seemed to be so sorry about the way they treated me before.

Michelle is describing how her youth seemed to stop some adults from believing in her symptoms and presuming that she had ulterior motives for the way she was behaving, rather than having a serious condition, like diabetes. I say "some adults," but it was actually those in a position of power and, while we can excuse teachers as seeing many different behaviors from children day in and day out, a reality in our ageist society is that the youth are dismissed because they are not respected as fully formed humans.

Ageism against older people has been and continues to be rampant, but the story of an older woman found in this chapter speaks both to ageism while, perhaps, also upholding it. At 64, Audrey is the oldest person that told their story and hers primarily focuses on how she is treated because of her strength and ability. Through her participation in CrossFit and many other sports, she defies expectations of what an older woman's body is supposed to be able to do or be seen doing. She was recounting how strangers in public spaces come up to her to acknowledge the unusualness of her physique:

I just get people coming up to me. In grocery stores. Shops. People chasing . . . I've had people chase me. They say, "Oh, my God, you look amazing." It's clear I'm older and I have a lot of muscle tone. It feels really kind of cool when you're in your 60s, right? That's not why I do it. I do have to stay fit because I want to compete. I don't care what I look like, as long as I can compete in my sport and do well, but the comments from others do make me feel proud of my strength.

60 Transforming Bodies

In one instance of Audrey's story, she says she has been referred to as a hero because of her commitment to exercise. This may seem like an entirely positive story, and for Audrey, it seems to be, but it also speaks to the ways that other bodies are also considered *less than*. If some bodies are valorized for being something unexpected, it also positions bodies that don't exceed expectations as not special, not good enough, not heroic. This reflects the complexity of ableism and ageism.

Dis/Ability and Explorations of Self

When we explore bodies as spaces of possibility, it opens up the ways that we can frame dis/ability to imagine what our bodies can do, or perhaps, what they desire. In Garland Thomson's (1997) discussion of extraordinary bodies, she says "[t]he ways that bodies interact with the socially engineered environment and conform to social expectations determine the varying degrees of disability or able-bodiedness, or extra-ordinariness or ordinariness" (7). Put more plainly, if we think about the relationship of our bodies to the environments around us, such as the stairs example earlier, we can better understand why some bodies are considered abled, while some others are disabled. Laura reflects on these realities in terms of the relationship of their ADHD (attention-deficit/hyperactivity disorder) and hiking:

One big thing for me personally is that I have ADHD. And when I'm hiking, it's a baseline – walking through nature and doing light orienteering, and the background stuff you need to do to keep yourself alive and on track, is a really, really good background stimulus that is just enough to keep me stimulated, while leaving enough space for me to do other things. And so, while I'm hiking, I can't just sit down and read a book, it doesn't work, my brain is not able to focus. But I can listen to a 15-hour audiobook in a single sitting while I'm hiking. I can just get up in the morning, put on the audiobook, and walk the whole day and listen to it and remember everything. And it's my favorite way of consuming books because it gives me that peace. So, I think a lot of it for me is just the activity itself, regardless of where exactly I am, is something that helps my body regulate itself better, and helps me help my brain be more focused and calm. I've always been into nature, I've always loved being in nature, just physically, I feel like my body belongs outside, and I don't like being inside at all. Like, if I have a chance, I will always be in fresh air. I will always be in the sun or in the rain, I don't care. And that's just how I always was from like, even as a kid. And I think part of that was an escape from society. It was an escape from gender, social expectations, and an escape into something that feels more natural and less destructive for how my brain works, I guess, in my experience of it at least. And so that was a way for me to get away from all of that. So honestly, I think for me, those are the biggest things. I mean, I love the views. It's brilliant, beautiful. That's really nice. But the main thing is the way it calms me when I'm hiking. And also just, it's a really special place that you get into after a while when consistently the only thing you really have to think about when I am outdoors is 'where do I sleep? What do I eat? What do I drink?' And that's it. It really simplifies your life. And I think especially right now, with everything happening around us, especially as a trans person in the United States. I'm really looking forward to more of that.

Celebrating our bodies, embracing our minds, and framing who we are as a journey to self-acceptance is something Laura and Jules express consistently in their stories. Not that they claim the journey is an easy one, but the ways that they both endeavor to connect with the aspects of themselves that are often rejected by normative social expectations is something to pause and reflect on:

It's interesting to be a part of a book that talks about how our bodies transform. I have a disability, which I rarely discuss. One of my legs is 3 inches shorter than the other – this is a result of many, many things we don't need to get into, but it impacts everything – my clothes, my shoes, my dancing on stage, pain I experience, my boy pants, my girl skirts, the whole thing. It has been transformative in how I think about the world around me and how I have tried to "fit" or, at least, I used to. I have totally let that go at this point. I love all the mis-fitting parts of me. I'm a drag artist after all!

(Jules)

As Garland Thomson (2009) notes,

[t]he people who inhabit such bodies are misfits in the literal sense of the word. Their unexpected bodies do not fit into a world built for others. Somehow their lives got set on the wrong stage, so that often their stories are as compelling as their sight.

(167)

Having a body that doesn't fit, both in the physical sense, such as in Jules' story, but perhaps also in the social sense when we include neurodivergence, such as in Laura's story, reemphasizes how dis/ability is the right way to frame these stories. Ability and disability must be paired because they are

62 Transforming Bodies

always shadowing each other in how we relate to ourselves and those around us. For example, at one point in my conversation with Anne, I asked her if she identifies as disabled. She said,

> *Hmmm. Do I? All of my anxieties, my skin picking. Yes, I guess it is a disability. It's a mental illness. It's a mental thing. I'm functional. Like, I may have all these things, but I'm highly functional. Yeah. I have PTSD (post-traumatic stress disorder), and I have generalized anxiety, panic attacks, depression, an eating disorder. It's who I am. It's what it is.*
>
> (Anne)

The acknowledgment of dis/ability is key here, because Anne notes that she is "functional," which is important to her identity as a partner, mother, member of society, and so on because we so often see those who are classified as disabled as problematically outside of the category of 'functioning' or 'normal.'

Lives, Interrupted

In Suleika Jaouad's (2022) beautiful memoir *Between Two Kingdoms: A Memoir of a Life Interrupted*, she references the Joan Didion line "we tell ourselves stories in order to live." Jaouad's mission in her book consistently highlights the importance of storytelling that can convey the horrific, peaceful, wonderful, mediocre, and devastating aspects of the human experience in relation to illness and pain. I was so inspired by Jaouad's book that I want to share two passages from it here and use this section of the chapter to prioritize the stories of the participants who echo some of her sentiments.

Jaouad tells the story of her leukemia journey that began in her early 20s. Through reflections on painful treatment, emotional and future upheaval, and the complexity of healing, her story speaks to how tumultuous illness and disability can be in a world that prioritizes a certain form of "normal" or "healthy" living. Jaouad (2022) says,

> There is no restitution for people like us, no return to days when our bodies were unscathed, our innocence intact. Recovery isn't a gentle self-care spree that restores you to a pre-illness state. Though the word may suggest otherwise, recovering is not about salvaging the old at all. It's about accepting that you must forsake a familiar self forever, in favor of one that is being newly born. It is an act of brute, terrifying discovery.
>
> *(234)*

Jaouad's story speaks to the ways that her life was interrupted by cancer. There was the time before and after diagnosis. The diagnosis itself became the boundary between who she was and who she is because of everything that has transformed her life since her relationship with cancer began.

Rachel's story also winds through her own experience with a life being interrupted. I present it here in much longer detail than some others so that the depth of her story comes through in her own words:

The thing about me is that basketball is a big part of my identity, I suppose. So, my first game at nationals in my final year of university, 19 seconds into the game, I tore my ACL. [Sidenote: The anterior cruciate ligament (ACL) is a ligament in the center of the knee that prevents the shin bone (tibia) from moving forward on the thigh bone (femur).] *I had no previous injuries. Before, I hurt some fingers and had bruises and stuff. But I had never missed a basketball game – in my whole life. I played my whole life. And then I had to sit out the whole national tournament in my final year. It was going to be my final tournament and the most important one of my basketball career. That was my catalyst for change, obviously, because I went from being like, at the top of my game, to not being able to walk in a moment, instant.*

This would have happened in March, but I didn't have my surgery until the end of October. In that time period, I was working at a limited capacity. So, some people tear their ACL and they can just get back up the next day and nothing bothers them, but I couldn't really straighten my leg fully and couldn't bend quite right. I could walk after about a week and a half. I was walking, but I couldn't run. I couldn't bend down. So, there was that period before surgery and I had gotten to a point where I was living my day-to-day life as I normally would. I was walking and doing other things. I just couldn't do sport. Then I got surgery.

And, it's funny because I knew this was happening, but you walk into the hospital, being able to walk around and your life is kind of normal, and then you leave wearing the full leg brace and not being able to walk.

The recovery, well it's kind of an intense process. It's usually anywhere between a 9- to 18-month recovery from the time you get surgery. It's a very long process. I was in a full leg brace locked straight for a couple of weeks, and then I was able to unlock it to certain positions. So, I basically had to relearn to walk. And then as you go, you're basically learning how to walk again; how to basically exist as a symmetrical human being because and I spent eight months sort of favoring one leg, so you have to unlearn so many habits because your brain and your body was just protecting itself.

Everyone warned me that it would be tough. But, I thought, "Well, that's fine. I'm tough too. I can handle it" . . . but it was definitely really tough.

So, I had my surgery at the very end of October of 2019. And then we all know, March 2020, there's a pandemic. I was kind of on the brink of almost being able to run. In order to do that, I had to do a lot of weight training to get the muscles around my knee back up strong, so I could protect myself. So, I was going to go to the gym three times a week doing exercises to strengthen it so I could get myself to running. I was still having pain, like not really fully being able to straighten my leg or Band Aid, like I was still in the early process. And then I got sent home. So, I couldn't go to the gym anymore. I found going to the gym quite hard, because it was the one thing that was making me better. But every time I did it, it reminded me of everything that I couldn't do. I think I also had a bit of self-pity being like, "Why did this happen? This shouldn't have happened to me".

I guess that would be one big change, because I went from being at the top of my game in terms of athletic performance to not being able to walk and then I spent really a full year and a half trying to recover. On top of that, a lot of athletes will gain weight, obviously, after they finish their sport. I kind of had this coupling of two things happening at once. I had this injury that was preventing me from walking and being able to do the things I normally do. But then also when I was in university, we were practicing six times a week, right? And then I was doing extra sessions like three or four times. I was exercising at a very intense rate multiple times a week – at least 10 or 12 times a week. So, I went from being so active and so able-bodied, to being not being able to do these things. It was who I was.

And then obviously your body changes, which is something I'm still dealing with accepting. ACL injuries are really hard for people to get through like mentally. And then there's also the ending of a basketball career in sport . . . it's a loss of identity. So, these all got smashed into one.

This is probably not the best story in terms of getting through and recovering from something. I feel like it's more pushed to the side in terms of how I am moving forward. But I do play basketball now. I would also consider myself fairly able. But I don't think I'll ever be . . . I don't think my body . . . the way it looks and the way it feels, but also the way it performs, that I'll ever get back to that place where I was. I know that it's possible. I just don't know if it ever will because it takes such a big commitment to get it back. So, I guess it was a weird time for me to go from, like I said, this peak performance to literally the worst my body has ever been in terms of looks, but also like feeling I am forever injured. Forever different.

(Rachel)

Reading Rachel's story, I can feel the loss of a core identity in her life. In our interview, she spoke of her family, her team, and her body in ways that showed how interconnected her ability to play basketball was with how she imagined herself and her relationship to other people. There was a before and an after. In particular, these passages from Rachel speak to the ways that she imagined her body before as well as after her injury: "I went from being so active and so able-bodied, to being not being able to do these things. It was who I was." She also says, "Feeling I am forever injured. Forever different."

Some may question how we can compare Rachel's story to Suleika Jaouad's story of leukemia, as Rachel's experience of dis/ability was not life-threatening, but our experiences of life being interrupted by dis/ability do not have to be framed in a binary of life or death in order for them to be meaningful, transformative stories to tell. They can be experiences full of physical and emotional calamities that change our lives in innumerable ways. As Jaouad (2022) reflects on her path to recovery (alongside a friend going through similar treatment), she says,

> Our bodies and thus our lives are capable of implosion at a moment's notice. In a way, setbacks were easier to deal with when we were still in treatment: We were prepared for the possibility that things could take a turn. But when the body betrays you again and again, it obliterates whatever nascent trust you've restored in the universe and your place in it. Each time, it becomes harder to recover your sense of safety. After you've had the ceiling cave in on you – whether through illness or some other catastrophe – you don't assume structural stability. You must learn to live on fault lines.
>
> *(273–4)*

For our purposes, the meaning of a fault line is something resembling a split or rift that may cause issues or problems. If we need to learn to live on fault lines then we can imagine ourselves transforming with caution, care, and perhaps a measure of preparation. I hope that the stories in this chapter convey how complicated it is to live in bodies that transform with age *and* how complicated it is to live in bodies that relate to dis/ability. I think that the stories expressed here convey caution, in terms of how to ready yourself for what might be to come – in the ways that the participants have been cautious and how their bodies changed in ways that they hadn't imagined. More importantly, I think that these stories demonstrate how much we often care for and love the bodies that we are in – even when they frustrate, betray, and surprise us. The lessons here seem to imply that we need to care for what bodies can offer us and how they might need different forms of caring over the course of our lives. In the next chapter, you will read about how first and last names can transform. These embodied transformations largely happen because there has been a fault line that led to a change in how people desire to classify their bodies.

66 Transforming Bodies

Key Terms

Ability – Ability is a socially constructed signifier for normal bodies; whatever is considered a 'normal body' in any particular cultural moment, space, or time will indicate to a culture what it means to have an 'able' body.

Ableism – Ableism is the discrimination of, and social prejudice against, disabled people based on the belief that typical abilities are superior. Ableism is rooted in the assumption that disabled people require 'fixing' and defines people by their disability. ·

Age – Age refers to a period of human life, measured by years from birth, usually marked by a certain stage or degree of mental or physical development and involving legal responsibility and capacity.

Ageism – Ageism refers to the stereotypes (how we think), prejudices (how we feel), and discrimination (how we act) toward others or oneself based on age.

Age Stratification – Age stratification refers to the ways that we hierarchically rank people into age groups within a society. These age groups are variable and are used for many purposes to create manufactured boundaries and lump certain people into groups based on a number that has very little to do with the reality of the lives of those in that group. It can also be defined as a system of inequalities linked to age.

Cishet – Cishet means someone who is both cisgender and heterosexual. It could also mean both cisgender and heteroromantic. In other words, a cishet person identifies as the gender they were assigned at birth, and they're attracted to people of the opposite gender.

Disability – Disability is a socially constructed identity that can be defined as a representation, a cultural interpretation of bodily difference, and a comparison of bodies that structure social relations and institutions.

Dis/Ability – Using a slash through the word disability, to create dis/ability emphasizes how much disability and ability rely on one another in order to exist. Disability cannot exist without ability and we can't understand either term without the other.

Youngism – Youngism refers to ageism toward younger adults and is fueled by the conflation of age with maturity and the misperception that an older age is required for competency.

Questions for Reflection and Discussion

1. As you can see so far from this book, the word *normal* comes up quite often. If you were to define that word for your own purposes, how would you characterize it? What can it be replaced with?
2. Rachel's story in this chapter might be challenging for some readers to engage with if they have never played sports or built their identities and

body around a major interest. Did you relate to Rachel's story – either for yourself or someone you know? What was similar? What was different?

3. When I read Suleika Jaouad's (2022) memoir *Between Two Kingdoms: A Memoir of a Life Interrupted*, I was overwhelmingly moved by her ability to convey the depths of her feelings and memories to her readers. It caused me to reflect on my own experiences and relationships to illness and ability. Are there any books or other stories that you have encountered that have caused you to think differently about your own body or your relationship to other people's bodies?

References

Applewhite, Ashton. 2016. *This Chair Rocks. A Manifesto Against Ageism.* New York: Celadon Books.

Clare, Eli. 2001. "Stolen Bodies, Reclaimed Bodies: Disability and Queerness." *Public Culture* 13 (3): 359–65. https://doi.org/10.1215/08992363-13-3-359.

Fritsch, Kelly. 2019. "Ramping Up Canadian Disability Culture." In *The Spaces and Places of Canadian Popular Culture*, edited by Victoria Kannen and Neil Shyminsky, 265–72. Toronto: Canadian Scholars Press.

Garland Thomson, Rosemarie. 1997. *Extraordinary Bodies: Figuring Physical Disability in American Culture and Literature.* New York: Columbia University Press.

———. 2009. *Staring: How We Look.* New York: Oxford.

Goodley, Dan. 2018. "The Dis/ability Complex." *Journal of Diversity and Gender Studies* 5 (1): 5–22.

Grealy, Lucy. 1994. *Autobiography of a Face.* New York: First Mariner Books.

Jaouad, Suleika. 2022. *Between Two Kingdoms: A Memoir of a Life Interrupted.* New York: Random House.

Kite, Lindsay, and Lexie Kite. 2021. *More Than a Body. Your Body is an Instrument, Not an Ornament.* New York: Harvest.

5
NAMES

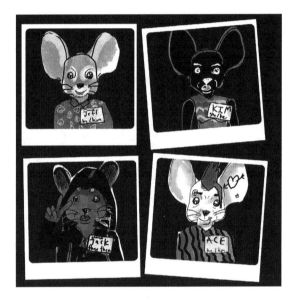

Names

FIGURE 5.1 *At first, I wasn't really certain how to showcase a change of name. So, I started picturing one of those meet and greet events if they were made of cool people. Everyone has a little name tag and there's a photo booth. The whole idea is to have these little Polaroids on a very plain background. Just kind of showing people expressing themselves through their image, but also through their name. Both are named, but that is in a physical form on their nametag. But the name also signifies who they are and how that name represents who they choose to be. It's also nice to include cute and adorable mice, because some of these topics are heavy! Again, I incorporated various forms of gender expression and you can come up with a whole backstory for each of these mice yourself. That's the fun part. (Damian)*

Damian Mellin, 2024

Names **69**

> *I have to pick my battles and I can fight the patriarchy in lots of different ways and break the binary, but this was just setting myself up for like repeated assumptions and misgendering [if I kept my original name]. So, that was the first thing I did – I changed my name to Ari.*
>
> (Ari)

> *My name isn't Jules, but I want you to use that here. Names are so critical. I have my [drag] stage name, my quote-unquote real name, and now Jules. They are all who I am.*
>
> (Jules)

When you think of your own name, does it capture who you are? Does your name connect with the ways you want people to engage with your body? Have you ever desired, or felt it necessary, to change your name? The history of changing a name is vast and far too complex to do justice to here. But let's recount some ways that names have been/are changed:

- Practices of colonization and genocide have resulted in the loss and replacement of Indigenous names.
- Many immigrants change their names in some way to assimilate into the language or naming practices of their new country and culture.
- Straight/heterosexual women have consistently changed their last names to take the last name of their husbands at the time of marriage and/or at the time of divorce. Historically, this was because their body became the property of their husbands. Prior to marriage, a woman's body used to belong to her father.
- Some people have their names changed for them or choose to change their names after being adopted into a new family.
- People choose usernames online that represent a version of our digital selves, whether it is the same name we use offline or an entirely new moniker.
- Trans people often change their names in order to align with the gender identity that they identify as.
- Disliking the associations that one's birth name offers, some have chosen to change either their first name, last name, or both in order to more closely align with their politics and/or gender identity.

This list is not exhaustive, but it does give a sense of some of the ways that people have had their names changed or chose to change them from the name they were given at birth. Our names are important markers of some elements of who we are. It distinguishes us as a unique person and serves as an identity marker to identify our bodies to ourselves. Charlotte Hagström explains that "we use names to gain knowledge about who a person 'is'" (81). The role

70 Transforming Bodies

of naming then, and considering the ways that we use language to identify ourselves and one another, is critical in thinking about how these names say something about our bodies. Because names and pronouns are two ways people call and refer to others, they are personal and important. **Pronouns** are words that can replace a noun in a sentence and we most commonly use them to replace a person's name and, often, to identify their gender. In English, our most commonly used pronouns (*he*/*she*) specifically refer to a person's gender. For queer, gender-nonconforming, non-binary, and transgender people, these pronouns may not fit with our bodily presentations, can create discomfort, and can also cause stress and anxiety when used incorrectly – whether intentionally or not.

Pronouns Are Political

Before we look at the importance of names, let's explore the role of pronouns in addressing the bodies, particularly the gendered bodies, of other people. Pronouns have always been political. While the discussions around them have been transforming fairly dramatically over the last ten years, a discussion of pronouns isn't new. As Lal Zimman (2016) writes,

> The major pronoun shift of the 20th century was undoubtedly the move away from the generic masculine – i.e., the use of "he" as the default pronoun to refer to a person whose gender is unspecified – and toward more inclusive/less androcentric options like s/he, he or she, the generic feminine (she), or singular they. There are a number of parallels between the changes currently happening with singular they and the processes through which feminists challenged the idea that the generic masculine was a grammatical accident free of politics.
>
> *(n.p.)*

Common pronouns include *she*/*her*/*hers*, *he*/*him*/*his*, and *they*/*them*/*theirs*. There are other nonbinary pronouns, such as *zie*/*zim* and *sie*/*hir*. As a professor, I often "teach" the lesson of why pronouns are important to students, colleagues, and those not in academia on a fairly regular basis. My explanation goes something like this:

> It is important to ask each person what their pronouns are – whether you think that you might know them or not – as we cannot visually tell how people identify. Their bodies do not tell us. When someone is referred to with the wrong pronoun, it can make them feel disrespected, invalidated, dismissed, alienated, or **dysphoric** (often all of the above). Asking someone's pronoun and offering yours is a practice of inclusion. Using **inclusive language** for 2SLGBTQIA+ youth and adults drastically decreases

experiences of depression, social anxiety, suicidal ideation, and other negative mental health factors.

A key reality check moment: It is a privilege to not have to worry about which pronoun someone is going to use for you based on how they perceive your gendered body. If you have this privilege, yet fail to respect someone else's gender identity, it is not only disrespectful and hurtful, but also oppressive. In the following, Jules and Laura explain how pronouns are related to their identity:

My pronouns are she and he and they. Why? Well, I am all of these things. It also makes it easier with all of the shitty people who want to hurt me and other queer **folx** *(Everyone should spell folx with an x please!). Fuck them. You can't hurt me by getting my pronoun wrong! Ha. Having said that, it totally sucks when people use the wrong pronouns or when the straights feel they don't need to use pronouns because it's obvious to everyone what your gender is. It is not.*

(Jules)

It's complicated for a lot of people, but not for me. I don't care. I think, like in everyday life, she is just what everybody uses, because that's just what I look like. That's my pronoun most of the time, when I'm at work, that's just what 95% of the time people use for me – she/her pronouns. And I don't mind that I've gone through a lot of different changes from she/her exclusively to she/they then they/them exclusively to anything. With friends and with my wife, and with a lot of other people who are in the community – for me, I honestly don't care and they can use whatever they want and can have fun with it. I don't think there's anything that I don't like. I'm at a point where nobody uses he/him pronouns for me, because they no longer recognize me as a man. . . . And so at this point, I don't care anymore. But for simplicity's sake, I usually put they or she, they/them and leave it at that.

(Laura)

As a cisgender woman, my pronouns are also key to my identity. I use she/her and when I have stressed the importance of pronoun use in various talks or teaching spaces, there has definitely been some pushback. The idea that everyone should share their pronouns has been met with criticism, but this is a very easy place where we can normalize inclusion. Just because my body seems to imply that my pronouns are she/her does not mean that that is true for other people. Everyone stating pronouns, especially cisgender people,

72 Transforming Bodies

acknowledges that the onus for inclusive practices should not be strictly placed on queer people.

The complexity of language, while also the comfort (and perhaps laziness) that people often express when they are asked to use pronouns that seem unfamiliar to them, such as they/them, is not an actual problem. The biggest argument people make about they/them pronouns is that, when used for one person, they are grammatically incorrect. But what people don't realize is that they use the singular 'they' all the time. In fact, I did it in this paragraph – "when they are asked to use pronouns that seem unfamiliar to them" – and it is clear that I can be referring to one person. It seems like the hesitancy is much more connected to the social constructions of gender that make they/them an issue, rather than a grammatical concern.

The embedded elements of gender in many languages are something that also adds complexity to this discussion, and while English does not have a grammatical gender as many other languages do, gender is often fundamental to how people relate to one another in English. This, however, is not universal. As Laura notes,

> *Because I'm Hungarian, I can tell you that Hungarian doesn't have grammatical gender in the way that the language really exists. Like, some languages have a lexical gender, so you have ways to use words that are defined as feminine or masculine or signify somebody's gender, but there's no he or she in Hungarian. There's no her or his, all of those things are the same. It just doesn't exist in the grammar.*

A gender-neutral language is possible but challenging, since so many of our practices still revolve around positioning gender as the primary identifier of each person. Pronouns themselves are not necessarily a consistent way to engage with someone's identity, however. Laura explains:

> *It seems that pronouns make people feel seen, but they are also a limiting factor. Because I mostly don't really care so much about pronouns being used, but I often struggled at first. I am really comfortable with who I am, but when I was younger, it was important. Less so now, but still, I'm kind of uncomfortable with it when people look at me, and I feel like they are putting me in a box. Pretty much regardless of what box they put me in. I don't like the fact that people gender me, I guess. And so, what I noticed is that as I was cycling through different pronouns that I would give people to use for me, they would react in a way where they almost felt like me telling them what my pronouns are, was me telling them what my gender identity is. Because pronouns are conflated with*

*identity and expression. And so, the reason I switched from saying she/
her to they/them to any pronoun at all was because I flipped that power
dynamic. Because when I tell you, it's she/her, then you feel like I told
you something about who I am. And that's not really the point. And
that's not really how it works for me. But when I tell you any and all
pronouns are fine, pick whatever you want, I'm putting you in a position
where now you have to pick a pronoun based on what you think. And
so now you're telling me something about what you think of me instead
of you feeling like I've told you something about what I think of myself.*

Laura is talking about relations of power and how closely they are tied to the
ways that we identify, as well as the ways that our bodies look. When they say,
"I flipped that power dynamic," it shows us how there is power embedded in
understanding ourselves and those around us. The ability to name and recognize that power dynamic is often a result of a multitude of experiences where
people feel disempowered or marginalized by the culture(s) in which they find
themselves. These power dynamics are even more obvious when we consider
changing your name once you transition your gender. Now that we know a bit
more about the importance and politics of names and pronouns, let's take a
closer look at how they affect and are affected by transforming bodies.

Being Trans, Changing Names

As a key element of identity, names, particularly first names, provide a point
in a trans person's life when they can transform a key element of who they
used to be into who they are. Our names give our bodies context and individuality. In 1975, Paul Tournier wrote *The Naming of Persons*, and he
writes that

> to change one's name is to break one's continuity as a person, to cut one-
> self off from the whole of one's past, which has defined one's person up to
> that point. Proof of this is the fact that a change of name may be desired
> by an individual and accepted by society when the change has a [social]
> significance. The new name asserts that a new life is beginning, like a new
> birth.
>
> *(19)*

This idea of a new beginning is true of any change of name, but for trans folx
it is (often) a key element in the ways that they want their body and their
identities to be recognized as they move through the world.

In a study of transgender youths and mental health, researchers led by a
team at the University of Texas at Austin, found that when transgender youths

74 Transforming Bodies

are allowed to use their chosen name in places such as work, school, and at home, their risk of depression and suicidal ideation drops. The authors say,

> [m]any kids who are transgender have chosen a name that is different than the one that they were given at birth. . . . We showed that the more contexts or settings where they were able to use their preferred name, the stronger their mental health was.
>
> *(Russell et al. 2018, 503)*

While a legal name change is often not available to these youth due to age or other constraints, the capacity for transgender youth to use and be recognized by their chosen name clearly has important implications for mental health. This is also true for adults. Ari, Haz, and Laura all explained their name stories in compelling ways. Let's read/hear from Ari first.

This was a really hard decision to change the name that I went by. So, my legal name was and is still Suzanne and I went by Suzi. And I was really torn about changing my name because there was nothing wrong with Suzi. The problem with Suzi is that other people heard it and then they knew I was a woman when they heard it. And so therefore had all of these assumptions about Suzi. And so, I worried that if I changed my name, I was basically just buying into those assumptions. I was reifying that, right? Like, why can't I be a genderqueer person and Suzi? Of course I can. But I have to pick my battles and I can fight the patriarchy in lots of different ways and break the binary but this was just, it just was setting myself up for repeated assumptions and misgendering. So, that was the first thing I did – I changed my name to Ari.

And I was looking for a name that could be used for boys or girls, men or women. That was part of it also. The way I picked my name is a story. My father was born in Iraq, and immigrated to the United States in the 1960s. And I learned, probably not until high school, or maybe even college, that my last name – Agha – was not my father's last name growing up. And I learned my family is actually of Iranian descent. And so, his original last name is very identifiably Farsi. And he was literally banned from going to college or to go to university with that name. They're like, you're an Iranian, you can't go to college. And so, he changed his last name to Agha.

And I was, of course, furious that this happened to him, and that this part of his identity, and my identity, therefore, was literally erased. And so already is a bit of an acknowledgment of that connection to that. And I think in some ways, probably at that time, subconsciously, it would make it easier for my dad to accept this kind of connection when

I chose Ari. And I also chose my mom's maiden name as my middle name, for the same reason that she's an only child. And, for you know, she took my dad's last name. So, I changed my name first. And that was the first thing I told people in the world. So family, friends, colleagues, all those kinds of things. And at the time, I said, you know, don't worry about pronouns, like, my pronouns aren't changing. And, and I was very . . . I acknowledged that I know, it's hard to imagine me with a new name and new pronouns. So, my attitude was "Don't worry about it, if you don't get it, right?" Then it was maybe two months later, where I followed this by an email saying, like, "I'm using them as my pronoun now". Yeah, it just felt like too much to ask for people to use a different pronoun and a new name at the same time.

Ari's story connects to many political realities of changing a name as a trans person. Traditionally, names are a historical sign of gender (as well as ancestry) and people still use birth names to indicate the gender of their newborn. Eric Plemons (2017) wrote *The Look of a Woman. Facial Feminization Surgery and the Aims of Trans-Medicine*, where they say

> [b]ecause woman is a social identity reserved almost exclusively for those occupying bodies read as female, so long as others see a trans-woman's body as a male body, she cannot accomplish the goal of her transition, which is to transform her identity from man to woman. (89)

While Plemons is specifically talking about transitioning from a man to a woman, the comparison beyond the form of transition is still apt. As Ari notes, being identified as Suzi prohibited the acknowledgment of Ari's gendered body as *not a woman*.

Laura's story of name change is similar to Ari's in terms of the way that Laura crafted a name that connected to their history and family.

I don't have a super complex story for my name. Honestly. My first name is Laura. I grew up bilingual Hungarian German, I spend most of my time in an English-speaking context, I also spend some time living in France and I speak French. And my previous name was a very short name that works in all of these different languages. It was a biblical name, which is always a nice shortcut for Western countries. And I wanted to have something similar again, my last name is something I always have to spell anyways – it doesn't matter where I am. And so, I decided I wanted to have a short name that everybody knows how to pronounce, and everybody knows how to spell. And that is part of all those languages. And those were honestly my only parameters. And then I just tried on different names for size. And at some point, was like, "Oh, what about Laura?" And I realized that works. Well, that feels good. There is also a name that I used for well over 10 years before I came out in any online context, when I would play a character in a video game, or whenever I would play a character without really thinking about why, I always played female characters. And I always called them Elizabeth. And so that's why that became my second name. And at this point, I use both Laura and Eliza very actively, together or separately. So, there's no big political reason behind it for me, but yeah, yeah. People recognize these and use them.

As seen in Ari and Laura's stories, when loved ones learn of a new name and gender transition, it is rare that there is an expectation that everyone will just accept it immediately. Some people do, some need more time, but the openness and acknowledgment of the transition are so important. Haz tells her naming story next, which includes an important caveat at the end:

I go by Haz. My birth name is Molly. And it was a good name for me for about 20 years. And then it was like, I think I need a new name to hold onto who I am a bit better.

And there was a while where I was kind of going by both names. And then I decided that we're just gonna go to Haz full time. And it isn't common; it is kind of an unusual name. I mostly picked it up from fanfiction communities talking about Harry Potter. Oh, which is now very complicated as a trans person.

I know a lot of trans people who have this problem and I sometimes do too, where we have chosen a new name that we don't like anymore. Maybe think to ourselves, "I kind of want a new one." And I go in and out of that. I don't think I'm likely to change from Haz. First of all, I don't think I'm likely to legally change my name. That just seems like a lot of hoops that I just don't need to go through. But it also makes it a little awkward, like, when I'm filling out job paperwork or something. I debate which name to use – this one I can probably go as Haz, but this one probably needs to be Molly. It depends on which ones are official and which ones aren't. So that's interesting to figure out.

My parents are 90% great about the gender stuff. Yeah. You know, it's whatever. Especially my mom, but that's what parents are. My mom especially is a little confused about some of the gender stuff. But she's not bad about it. Like it could be a lot worse.

When Haz says that *"[i]t could be a lot worse,"* he is referring to the proliferation of **transphobia** that exists toward trans people. It can seem quite contentious when trans people select a new name – as if they are rejecting the life that they were given by their parents. This rejection of a birth name can be taken as an offense or is seen to be laborious for those around them – both legally and personally. This complexity can sometimes result in a new name being rejected and people intentionally denying the new name exists. As Taylor Koles (2024) argues, deadnaming is a term that started in the trans community to describe when a trans person is called by a name they no longer use, primarily in terms of the name that they used or that was given to them before their transition. When that former name is used, it is called their "deadname," and it can be considered derogatory. If you recall, Laura does not state their previous name, while Ari and Haz are comfortable outwardly acknowledging both names. This is a personal and political decision that must be respected.

Being Political, Changing Names

For some people, the name that they were given at birth may not suit their needs, for reasons that could be outside of their relationship to gender. We see this most commonly with celebrities and other artists, who often have a stage name or a pseudonym they use as performers. This is completely normal to most people. When activists change their name because its connotations – whether its origins or meanings – are not aligned with one's politics, a name can be framed as a political decision. This is not to say, of course, that changing one's name because they are trans is somehow apolitical, but to change it strictly for political motivation is something to explore.

Onomastics is the study of the etymology, history, and use of proper names. In the philosophy of language, a proper name – examples can include the name of a specific person or place – is a name which is used to uniquely identify its referent in the world. In a discussion of naming practices, William Bright (2003) argues that

> we need to realize that many people in the world do not have such highly organized systems of personal naming as we are accustomed to. . . . In European societies, as well as China and Japan, every person is assigned a public, legal name, in written form, around the time of birth; part of this usually reflects the child's father's name. The individual normally has that same legal name through life – with exceptions, e.g., where married women take on their husband's family names. In addition, a person may have informal "nicknames" during different parts of life. Sometimes

78 Transforming Bodies

these are used only by close relatives or intimates; in any case, they do not replace the public and legal names.

(672)

Here, it is clear that conventions of naming may not be universally accepted, however, they are primarily gendered.

James Scott, John Tehranian, and Jeremy Mathias (2002, 18) argue that last names or surnames "represent an integral part of knowledge-power systems" and are "a modern invention" linked with state control over people through legal systems and ownership of property – primarily through the last names of men. These gendered practices are also inherently colonial ones. Colonial practices in Canada and other colonial countries used "Western" naming systems to enforce the colonial practice of naming with little understanding and ability to accommodate diverse cultural practices, particularly Indigenous peoples' naming customs. For example, the colonial priority of creating fixed surnames not only destroyed the fluidity of Indigenous names, which are rooted in complex family naming systems, but also erased gender identities and communal sharing of land. These were often referred to as "civilization" projects. Rod Hagen (2015) notes that in 1935, Inuit people in Canada were initially issued 'dog tags' bearing an identification number, a practice abandoned in 1969, which was then replaced with 'Project Surname.' This colonial practice forced Inuit to use a surname in order for legislative convenience, creating a modern 'homogeneous' Canadian identity. Hagen (2015) also highlights the difference in the naming system, noting that while Anglo-Australian naming systems use names for identification: "Aboriginal communities 'names' convey very different information, such as status, kinship relationships, the relationship of the speaker to the person named and current personal circumstances of the individual concerned" (n.p.).

Activism that resists a legacy of colonial practice can take many forms and one of them is the reclamation of language and identity. Ra'anaa Yaminah Ekundayo, who has transitioned away from their last name 'Brown' in order to avoid its colonial implications, describes the ways that their connection to their former last name no longer fit with how they understood themselves:

My parents spent so long naming me and my siblings and we all have Arabic and African first names and middle names. But, my former last name – Brown – I always hated it. It's so generic. It's the ugliest color and then the more I did research on it, I discovered it comes from a European background. This is some colonial bullshit. But then I was like, okay, maybe I'll change my last name. And at one point, I was like, I'll just get married and change my last name then, but I'm no longer holding out hope for the institution of marriage because it's ridiculous.

*So, I started looking into it and a lot of my family comes from Jamaica.
And I was like, okay, what's the most common last name in Jamaica?
Fun fact. It's Brown. Yeah, joke's on me. I don't want that. And the
more I did work with BLM [Black Lives Matter], I wanted to know
more about myself and what it means to be a displaced person in the
African diaspora. I was also in a place of not knowing what it means to
be Jamaican and not knowing what it means to be of African descent.
My grandparents did this 23andme thing and apparently, we have a huge
Nigerian heritage. I know nothing about Nigeria, but I have a friend
who just slowly started learning about Nigeria. And then to my parents,
they got our names from this book about names for Arabic and African
children and I picked it up one day. And I recognized that I really just
wanted to change my last name to something meaningful. And I saw the
last name – Ekundayo – and I realized that it means sorrow becomes
happiness or joy. And I just felt like I was at this place in life where I was
finding happiness and what it means to me to be Black. So, it's something
that I'm always kind of questioning and even though I grew up in a very
multicultural place, I wasn't as aware of my Blackness.*

*And this is gonna sound so silly, but even in the process of choosing
a name, I was like, "Is it a good idea? I'm gonna make a mistake". And
then I just heard something about a lot of the people that I try to emu-
late in my work, who I read a lot of – like Assata Shakur, Angela Davis,
Stokely Carmichael, Malcolm X. And, all of them, at some point in their
activist career, all changed their names. Most chose Arabic names and
I'm already there, but whatever. But I find it so interesting how we go
through this . . . what I've been calling my racial awakening, or this radical awakening. When I realized this name – Brown – no longer fits this
body and this queer, Black activist identity that I am now possessing. So,
what does it mean to be able to rename yourself and give yourself this
identity that you couldn't speak to when you were a baby? I mean, you
don't know who you are when you are young, right? And you're trusting
your parents to give you that identity. And so now I found this identity
and I can ask, "What does it mean to possess this for me"?*

Politicizing our names is, perhaps, a new concept for some of you reading/
listening to this story. Ra'anaa is an activist and artist who embraces transformation and has an openness to new ideas. This can be a challenging reality
for some, but as Ra'anaa says,

*It's really important to find yourself and then your people (or do so at
the same time). The second I started to be able to say these things and
actually accept who I am and how I see the world, I really found this*

80 Transforming Bodies

cool group of people. And I realized that we don't have to worry about other people. Because at the end of the day, I am a Black person. And people are still gonna look at me and be like: there is a Black person who is doing all of these amazing things. I could also say nothing and still be perceived as this dangerous Black person who's angry. And so, my approach is, if you're gonna call me angry, here's why I'm angry. Yeah. Now you should be intimidated by me because I'm doing shit. I'm gonna change the fucking world. As a piece of advice, no matter how they – whoever they are – perceive you, it doesn't matter. Do what you're gonna do and be the person you want to be. And never peak. And that's one of the things I'm leaning into is to never peak. Life just gets better and it gets more sweet.

No matter what prompts a name change for someone, it is a profound and transformational decision to make about the labeling of one's body. It is not a superficial adjustment, and whether or not someone shares their motivations for changing their name, it is important to recognize that this decision was met with much thought and consideration. In Ra'anaa's earlier advice, creating a circle of support with like-minded people who recognize you for who you are is integral to our sense of self and what we see as possible for us to do in our lives.

Names That We Get to Choose

This chapter began with a quote from Jules saying,

My name isn't Jules, but I want you to use that here. Names are so critical. I have my [drag] stage name, my quote-unquote real name, and now Jules. They are all who I am.

It is an interesting thing when you offer people the chance to choose a name in an instance where they can create an anonymized identity for themselves. Sometimes they are unsure and need to take time to craft it, sometimes they have a name immediately ready, and sometimes they are completely unsure and want someone else to decide. It's perhaps more interesting because these are fairly low-stakes names, yet it takes time to ponder what this new name might be, even if it is only ever used in this one instance, in an academic book. But, here, these names are who these people are to us. There is no image of them. Just their words, connected to a name – one that might be theirs in 'real life' or might only appear here.

Considering then, the stories that appear in this chapter, name changes are so integral to how bodies are framed, demarcated, and held in our minds when we imagine our relationship to other people, that it is no wonder that a change of name can be destabilizing. But it is our hope that through these stories, it is also clear that a change of name can be empowering, self-actualizing, and the start of a new identity in someone's life. Names are part of our performance of self and, in the next chapter, we consider some visual elements of those performances – hair, fashion, and tattoos.

Key Terms

Dysphoric – To be dysphoric refers to experiencing dysphoria. Dysphoria is a profound state of unease or dissatisfaction. It is the opposite of euphoria. In a psychological context, dysphoria may accompany depression, anxiety, or agitation. Gender dysphoria is often used as an example.

Folx – Folx is a different way of writing *folks* that emphasizes the fact that you intend the word to include all groups of people. The spelling *folx* has been adopted by some as an explicitly inclusive term, intended to include groups that are typically marginalized, especially those from the 2SLGBT-QIA+ community.

Inclusive Language – Inclusive language is the words and phrases that can be used to avoid biases, slang, jokes, and other expressions that discriminate against groups of people based on race, gender, social class, ability, and so on.

Onomastics – Onomastics is the study of the etymology, history, and use of proper names.

Pronouns – A pronoun is a word that is used instead of a noun or noun phrase. Pronouns refer to either a noun that has already been mentioned or to a noun that does not need to be named specifically. Pronouns are how we identify ourselves and each other apart from our names.

Transphobia – Transphobia refers to negative attitudes, feelings, or actions towards transness and transgender people. Transphobia can include fear, aversion, hatred, violence or anger towards people who do not conform to normative gender roles.

Questions for Reflection and Discussion

1. At the beginning of this chapter, I asked: When you think of your own name, does it capture who you are? Does your name connect with the ways you want people to engage with your body? Have you ever desired, or felt it necessary, to change your name? Try to answer some of these.
2. Take a moment to Google some of the controversies surrounding pronoun use. Why do you think it is such a contentious or controversial subject?

3. Do you know the etymology or history of your first or last name? Do you think that is important for you to know? Why or why not?

References

Bright, William. 2003. "What is a Name? Reflections on Onomastics." *Language and Linguistics* 4 (4): 669–81.

Hagen, Rod. 2015. "Traditional Australian Aboriginal Naming Processes." *Proof of Birth*, untitled (futureleaders.com.au).

Hagström, Charlotte. 2012. "Name Me, Naming You. Personal Names, Online Signatures and Cultural Meaning." *Names and Identities, Oslo Studies in Language* 4 (2): 81–91.

Koles, Taylor. 2024, forthcoming. "The Semantics of Deadnames." *Philosophical Studies*. https://doi.org/10.1007/s11098-024-02113-x.

Plemons, Eric. 2017. *The Look of a Woman. Facial Feminization Surgery and the Aims of Trans-Medicine*. Durham and London: Duke.

Russell, Stephen T., Amanda M. Pollitt, Gu Li, and Arnold H. Grossman. 2018. "Chosen Name Use is Linked to Reduced Depressive Symptoms, Suicidal Ideation, and Suicidal Behavior Among Transgender Youth." *Journal of Adolescent Health* 63 (4): 503–5. https://doi.org/10.1016/j.jadohealth.2018.02.003.

Scott, James C., John Tehranian, and Jeremy Mathias. 2002. "The Production of Legal Identities Proper to States: The Case of the Permanent Family Surname." *Comparative Studies in Society and History* 44 (1): 4–44.

Tournier, Paul. 1975. *The Naming of Persons*. New York: Harper.

Zimman, Lal. 2016. "Pronouns Have Always Been Political." *Medium*, August 26, 2016.

6
PERFORMANCES

Performances

FIGURE 6.1 *How I grew up really influenced this. In my younger days, when I was cool, I was hanging out with a lot of drag kings. I was surrounded by activists but they had a very sexy kind of way of putting themselves out there in ways that we're trying to be shocking. Trying to rattle the system. I wanted to show people who are amplified. So, in this imaginary world where animals control everything and the world is just populated with animals, these birds are really showcasing who they are and how they want to express. Funky tattoos, outlandish outfits, performing on the mic on a random roof. I wanted this to be a bedrock of fun and creativity.* (Damian)

Damian Mellin, 2024

DOI: 10.4324/9781003380061-6

My body transformations relate, of course, to my top surgery, but I also have tattoos. I have a lot of tattoos. I have a half sleeve; I have a full sleeve. And I've got one leg pretty extensively covered. So, especially in the summer, people will stop me and they'll comment on that, too.

(Maria)

I'm very self-conscious about my hair. I used to have nice long hair. It was fine. But then what do you do when you don't have that anymore? After the chemo, it is very thin. I lost my hair, lost all my eyebrows, lost all my hair. And as you can see, it has never grown back. I only have eyebrows, I only have about a third of my eyelashes back. And they'll probably never come back. So, my story is, and then my story really is about the fact that because my hair never came back, people were looking at me differently.

And it drives me bananas because it doesn't matter if I have a nice sweater or something or nice earrings, because all you see is this shiny little scalp. And, it was even worse during COVID and when we were all on Zoom, because you're sitting there and you see yourself on the screen. So, the last three years have been horrible, because I sometimes dream and I think I'm cool. And I wake up and I realize, "Oh, I'm not me anymore". Because I can see my hair isn't there anymore.

(Amelia)

Hair, fashion, tattoos. These are not the only ways that we perform (makeup, jewelry, etc. are all relevant), but the realities of hair, fashion, and tattooing are the key ways that the participants talked about the presentation of their bodies as gendered artifacts. As Orbach says, "[a]s we perform our exercises, do our hair, put on our clothes, we are underpinning how we wish to be seen and how we see ourselves" (2009, 9). The participants also used these three elements to explore how they project and reclaim their bodies in the presence of other people.

Contemporary scholars of language and identity draw on Erving Goffman's (1959) work found in *The Presentation of Self in Everyday Life*, to outline a solid base for the idea of identity as a performance. Goffman explores the way in which individuals interact day-to-day using the metaphor of the stage and performers. Goffman writes that identity is an act of performance that asks that when an individual plays a part, they implicitly request observers to take seriously the impression that is fostered before them. The audience is asked to believe that the character they see actually possesses the attributes the performer appears to possess (Goffman 1959).

When applied to gender, we call this **gender performativity**. Gender performativity is a term first used by Judith Butler in their 2006 book *Gender Trouble: Feminism and the Subversion of Identity*. They argue that being born male or female does not determine behavior, rather we learn to behave

Performances **85**

in particular ways to fit into gendered society. Important for our purposes here, Butler's work allows for a widespread recognition that the idea of gender is an act, or performance – even if both these are conscious and unconscious decisions. This act is the way a person can walk, talk, dress, and behave based on what they see other gendered bodies doing. Butler's theory enables us to understand that what society regards as a person's gender is just a performance made to please or meet social expectations and not a true expression of the person or their gender identity.

When we think about how we present ourselves or perform our identities for one another, it is important to consider how performance markers allow other people to recognize what it is we are trying to convey with our gendered body. In Plemons's (2017) book on facial feminization surgery (FFS), they argue that these procedures can reshape the features of a face to achieve a more feminine, gender-affirming appearance:

> We don't all look the same under our haircuts, cosmetics, and T-shirts. We don't all have the same body shape with which we walk, gesture, dance, and talk ourselves into gendered distinction. Overwhelmingly the patients who sought FFS did so because these other mechanisms for enacting gender through doing – haircuts, cosmetics, T-shirts, walking, gesturing, dancing, talking – did not do for them what they hoped.
>
> *(129)*

The ability to recognize and be recognized by others is a standard of daily performance that most people want to participate in. I have only been misgendered once in my life (as far as I am aware) and it was a surprising, unsettling experience. We generally expect people to recognize what we are doing and to then treat us in the ways we expect. Jules, the only participant who identifies as a performer, spoke about performance and gender in an interesting way:

> *Doing drag gives you an interesting perspective on what is real or authentic. I literally transform every day, but doesn't everyone? When I get out there, I'm a woman. I look like a woman, I use a woman's name, I dress like a woman, I do my hair like a woman. Isn't the performance what makes us who we are? When I am on that stage, I am my drag persona. When I leave that stage, it's just a performance of a less public kind. I am still me and I am still performing.*

Jules is accounting for the ways that we are all performing, but also there is an undercurrent of a discussion of belonging. As Orbach (2009) says, "[w]

86 Transforming Bodies

herever we are, we seek belonging through our bodies" (168). Belonging is not always clear, however; sometimes we wish to resist belonging or being aligned with a certain group, category, or box that we feel we don't belong in. Discussions of hair, culture, and gender all speak to this.

Hair

In my previous book, *Gendered Bodies and Public Scrutiny* (2021), I wrote extensively on the politics of hair because two of the body stories centered on hair as an intersectional experience with strangers and comments – being a bald woman and being a Black woman. In that book, I started the section by saying, *Our hair is serious*. There are many parallels between my discussion there and here because our hair is inherently a space of transition and change over the course of our lives. Hair is seemingly mundane – we wash it, style it, cut it, and so on – these are also transformative acts. Our hair is also

> our glory, our nemesis, our history, our sexuality, our religion, our vanity, our joy, and our mortality. It's true that there are many things in life that matter more than hair, but few that matter in quite these complicated, energizing, and interconnected ways.
>
> *(Benedict 2015, xvii)*

As Elizabeth Benedict implies in this quote, our hair is political. For example, while an absence of hair for women can be a signal of illness or aging (as Amelia shares earlier), intentional baldness can also be a sign of fierce resistance to feminine norms. Hair is ultimately an expression of politics, personal beliefs, and a reflection of trends, fads, rebellion, and artistry. Rachael Gibson, a hair historian, was quoted in *Vogue India* as saying,

> Afro styles became intrinsically linked with civil rights, as natural hair came to be viewed as an important symbol of the movement and its "black is beautiful" ethos; skinheads represented rebellion and rejection of traditionally accepted social aesthetics in the 1980s; and the hair powder tax of 1786 led to mass rejection of wigs for men and brought in a new movement of short, natural hairstyles.
>
> *(Burney 2019)*

As signs of protest against expectations of gendered modesty, many women have cut or shaved their hair as a form of public protest – at times, risking their lives to do so.

At one point in telling their story, Ra'anaa says, "Everything I do with my body can be a statement. Bra, no bra. The way I style my Black hair. How people comment on it. If I wear makeup or not. That in itself is a statement."

The kinds of hair we have – how it looks, how it feels, its thickness or thinness, where it is, where it isn't, its color(s), and style – these are all embedded within gendered and racialized assumptions of hair goodness and desirability.

> And there are the other questions that hair leads to as well, about femininity, questions that haunt women of all shades, hues, and races. Why do we have to live under the tyranny of a global doctrine that posits femininity in the length and straightness of a woman's hair?
>
> *(Golden 2015, 30)*

Marita Golden (2015) argues that Black women – like all women – "live imprisoned by a cultural belief system about beauty and hair whose time should have passed" (31). Here, she is referring to how systemic privileging of white femininity – pale skin; European features; straight, long hair – have been and are still upheld as the colonial ideal of beauty. She goes on to say that "[l]ike everything else about Black folk, Black people's – and especially Black women's – hair is knotted and gnarled by issues of race, politics, history, and pride" (19).

There is an undeniable daily reality of hair – whether you have it or don't – that relates to how we perceive ourselves and how we imagine others perceive us. In Alane's case, when she lost her hair through chemotherapy treatments, she approached baldness matter-of-factly:

> *On the 16th day of my chemo treatment, I can remember being in the shower and washing my hair and seeing it all slowly get tangled in my fingers and then down the drain. But, you know, that didn't bother me that much. I mean, I was completely bald. And I had a lot of people who tried to help. I have a sister-in-law that knits a lot, and she made me some nice hats and things like that. But after a while, I decided that I was just done with that. So, I just went around bald everywhere. I went to work bald and I just wore nice earrings. So, that didn't really bother me. I have thought about if for any reason, if the cancer came back and I'd have to do it again, I'd be fine with the bald part.*

If you Google "women and baldness," it is very unlikely that you will find any resource on empowerment or resistance, but rather the majority of results speak about loss and shows sad-faced stock images of women identifying a lack of hair somewhere on their head. Of course, the gendered presentation of women, even women with short hair, is the expectation that they have some hair on their head and if they don't, it is likely that they "lost" it. Women's body hair removal – armpits, legs, facial, and pubic hair – however, is not something seen to be a personal loss, but framed as expected grooming.

88 Transforming Bodies

The discussion of removing body hair is fascinating and can be explored in more detail by reading Breanne Fahs' 2022 book, *Unshaved: Resistance and Revolution in Women's Body Hair Politics.*

As Ari discusses, when they initially came out as a lesbian, this new, transformed identity gave them a freedom to perform their identity in ways less constricted by the rules of femininity. This involved removing a lot of their hair. Ari says,

> *Identifying as a lesbian gave me room to sort of inhabit my body and express myself in ways that I had always wanted to do. It was maybe six months or nine months after I came out, I chopped all my hair off. Before that, I had really long hair and it went down to the middle of my back. It seems silly, but without the hair I could buy clothes sold in the men's department. And that actually was incredibly freeing, and incredibly liberating. Other than my hair, there were no other modifications that happened then. But it just felt really, really free. But it's because I had felt like it was okay, I had this permission, this space to present myself and see myself in a way that I just didn't have before.*

Resistance to expectations of hair is not easy. As Amelia says in the opening of this chapter: "I'm very self-conscious about my hair. I used to have nice long hair. It was fine. But then what do you do when you don't have that anymore?" I can attest that Amelia is, of course, a beautiful woman – inside and out – but she seems to express the belief that the loss of her hair equated with the loss of her femininity and beauty, particularly through how she imagines others see her. As she says, "[M]y story really is about the fact that because my hair never came back, people were looking at me differently" (Amelia). This idea that people are staring at Amelia for her hair loss is disheartening, but it is also not surprising. As Garland Thomson (2009) says,

> Because we come to expect one another to have certain kinds of bodies and behaviors, stares flare up when we glimpse people who look or act in ways that contradict our expectations. Seeing startlingly stareable people challenges our assumptions by interrupting complacent visual business-as-usual.
>
> *(6)*

We look at each other or, more pointedly, we stare at each other when something unexpected comes into view. At times, we ask questions of each other, but mostly, we offer a stare. This is true not only for our hair but also for how we dress and tattoo ourselves.

Fashion

Our gendered bodies are often tied to the idea that certain clothes are appropriate for certain times in our lives, occasions, sizes, and ages. What we wear when we are 5 years old is often not the same type of clothing that we wear at age 25 or 85. According to Susan B. Kaiser (2012),

> Fashion materializes as bodies move through time and space. Time and space are both abstract concepts and contexts: the process of deciphering and expressing a sense of who we are (becoming) happens in tandem with expressing when and where we are.
>
> *(1)*

The terms *fashion* and *clothing* tend to be used interchangeably, but they actually mean different things. **Fashion** conveys artistry, meaning, and intention, whereas clothing is the raw materials that a person wears. Fashion, in this sense, provides added value to clothing, as a form of self-expression. Clothing are simply the things that you wear to cover your body. Fashion itself is not visible in the clothing, but it is in the invisible elements that we use to express our identities to one another. The ways we express our connection with fashion merges us with our emotional needs; it expresses our inner individual personality through using color, shapes, symbols, brands, and other status items. Fashion is always at once public and private, material and symbolic. For some, fashion could be considered a chore, and they would rather simply think of clothing as functional, but for others, fashion is intimately tied to their expression of self.

Jules, as a drag performer, has thought considerably about his relationship to fashion:

> *When I am in a beautiful dress, covered in sequins, I feel alive and gorgeous. But I also feel alive and gorgeous when I am wearing a double-breasted suit. I feel gorgeous in different ways, but I am an icon, so that's why. When I was a little boy, I would try on my mom's dresses in secret. I was convinced that I needed to hide that part of myself. Live in shame, but I would also look at myself and see how beautiful I could be. I'm also handsome. I can hold both and fashion allows me to hold both.*

Fashion is an entire field of academic study, but the key for our purposes here is to consider how bodily transformation for the participants relates to fashion. For Haz, fashion and clothing are political, but they are also places of gendered contention:

90 Transforming Bodies

And the only thing that's been frustrating is about clothing. I mean it's just that when my body was changing, I was pretty rapidly gaining weight for about two or three years. And so, I was constantly having to change my clothes because of my size fluctuations and that was frustrating. But I didn't like to complain about it. I didn't want to be negative about it; I didn't want to be negative about my weight gain. Even if it wasn't directly about my weight gain, it was about having to buy new clothes all the time and growing out of clothes that I liked. But so, in some ways, I'm glad I've settled at this higher weight. Just because I don't want to have to keep buying new clothes. But I'm also wearing fairly loose, flowing dresses now, so if I gained 20 or 30 more pounds, I probably wouldn't have to change my wardrobe that much. So, I'm happy to stick with dresses.

The politics of size, particularly when our bodies are deemed "plus-size," render some clothes to be specialty and, often, more challenging to locate as well as more expensive to buy. Haz addresses this in the earlier quote, when they note how dresses easily accommodate changing size fluctuations, even if they don't meet the gendered presentation Haz might desire. As Deborah A. Christel and Susan C. Williams Née Dunn (2018) claim,

[t]here are rarely words used to classify non-plus size clothing because, anything other than plus-size is considered the norm, standard, regular or in-group. The importance of being thin is perpetuated by fewer plus-size clothing options, and this practice maintains the power of who can and cannot participate in certain fashions. (342)

Wearing loose-fitting dresses is a challenge for Haz but seems to be the only affordable and fashionable item of clothing that currently feels within reach for him. In terms of their gender presentation, Haz would rather have more options because he feels his identity is currently connected with being a man, and dresses do not align with that presentation. They explain:

At this point, I lean more towards male, but I'm not presenting male at all. And I think most of that has to do with perception because it would take a while before I was perceived as a man by other people. So, I'm not even going to try. But, it's okay – I'm comfortable. I like wearing dresses. I wear dresses basically every day right now. And I find that comfortable dresses are cute, among other things, in a way that men's clothing never gets quite as cute as a dress does. And I even have a dress that has he/him

all over with transgender pride colors, so that I love that one. It confuses
people and I do sometimes like that about it.

(Haz)

Clothing is politicized largely due to the fact that clothes are not just a form of art, but that they are wearable art. Particularly in the West, fashion can serve as a medium to criticize and comment on the mainstream, express individuality, and allow individuals to align themselves with marginalized groups, subcultures, and countercultures. Because it is literally embodied, clothing is a particularly unique form of interpersonal communication. Our fashion and the forms our clothing takes may often change; however, it is nearly always attached to our bodies in public – at any given moment signaling various aspects of our tastes and behaviors. While we may not all wear things with identifiers, such as a dress printed with him/him all over it, it is inevitable that clothes say something about their wearer.

Fashion is key to the ways many participants discussed how they want the world to see them, as well as how they have changed their fashion over the course of their lives to reflect their transforming body, image, and identity. For example,

My new thing is making t-shirts on the Cricut and you can just put spicy catchphrases on them to wear. So, my grandma's 80th birthday and her celebrations are this weekend. I realized that I needed to make a t-shirt because this would be the first time since pre-pandemic that I'm around this much of my family. But I know that there's a bunch of people in my family who might shit bricks if I wore a shirt that said Defund the Police! So, instead I was thinking of doing something that said 'Keep the farm out of the streets' or something fun like that. They might think I'm a vegetarian. Go ahead. And then I settled on a Fred Hampton shirt that I made that says 'I'm a revolutionary'. Like you get it if you get it, and if you don't, you don't. It's perfect. I want to make a statement, but intentional and I think grandma will like that. It's pretty great. My new thing is that I love making my family feel weird to me. Like, I can see them thinking, "Why are you doing that?" And I'm just like, packing all the makeup, packing all the face gems. And I'm like, what are they gonna say to me? Like, I'm on track to get my PhD. I feel like I've really earned this and I deserve this. And like, what are they going to do?

(Ra'anaa)

92 Transforming Bodies

It's almost impossible to find anything sexy or desirable in a bra made for a one-breasted woman. They are kept in the back of the bra store, away from the sexy normal bras. They always seem medical and boring.

(Amelia)

I always am worried about getting back to that bigger size to the point where I keep the jeans that were size 14 or 16. I keep all those clothes and like, again, I know size doesn't matter. It's the fit. It's whatever fits your body. But my hips don't lie. My hips don't lie. Sometimes I need a bigger size. It doesn't matter. It's my body and I'm okay with that. I'm good at that now. I keep those larger jeans though. Just in case.

(Anne)

I have my insulin pump already as a sticker on my body. So, I've dealt with that even before the continuous glucose monitor. One time I was at the pool, wearing a bathing suit, and a child pointed at me and said, "What is that?" And I'm not typically anxious about it in any shape or form. I'm not that self-conscious about it. But in that exact moment, it kind of was. I was at a pool – already a place where you might feel more vulnerable. So, I do get questions. But when I worked at a shoe store, I had a couple of people come up and actually physically poke it without asking me when it was showing. So that was uncomfortable. But I also get more questions about my insulin pump than the one on my arm, because not many people see it during the wintertime. It's more of a summer thing since my clothing shows my body more.

(Michelle)

Don't let me get started on gender and bathing suits, honey. I will never stop talking.

(Jules)

Any discussion of fashion and clothing could go on endlessly. Clothes are a necessity that most of us have strong feelings about. I am a lover of fashion, but I also have a 38″ inseam – not very easy to accommodate. What is most important about our stories of fashion and its connection to identity seem to be connected to how fashion is a crucial aspect of human existence, influencing the way we each present ourselves to the world and communicate our identities. Clothing choices can reflect the changes in our lives in terms of personal ideas regarding gender, as well as tastes, beliefs, values, and cultural backgrounds, making fashion a powerful tool for expressing one's identity.

Tattoos

In our current culture, it seems unusual when people younger than 50 years old do not have tattoos. Tattooing as a form of expression, while much more commonplace than it once was, is simply another element of embodied change. Orbach (2009) claims that "there has never been a 'natural' body: a time when bodies were untainted by cultural practices" (165). Bodies are modified and transformed from their natural state on a daily basis. We cut our hair and our nails, and many of us dye our hair and paint our nails, but we, as a society, also have entire professional fields whose work it is to permanently and surgically alter our forms for a wide array of reasons – some deemed medically necessary, some cosmetic, and some a combination of both. **Body modification** refers to the "physical alternation of the body through the use of surgery, tattooing, piercing, scarification, branding, genital mutilation, implants, and other practices" (DeMello 2014, 209).

These modifications or transformations can be temporary or permanent, such as piercings versus tattooing. There are many theories as to why people participate in practices of body modification and the histories of these traditions are varied across cultures and subcultures around the world. But the current reality is that tattoos are trendy. Mary Kosut (2006) refers to them as an "ironic fad," since tattooing was once seen as deviant behavior in Western culture, for it to now be so mainstream that it has lost most of its "edge" is, therefore, ironic. Deborah Davidson (2017) claims that tattooing is primitive and modern, a way of using our bodies as visual texts, which can function as sites of public storytelling and a tactile archive. As we know, identity formation and belonging can manifest in a variety of forms, and body modification is merely one of them.

Tattooing can also be considered a human self-retouching impulse borne out of various desires. Intentions can be symbolic, traditional, a historical document or a reference point, resistive, political, artistic, intimate, frivolous, performative, tributary, and more. Similarly, reactions to tattooing as a practice of identity formation can be awe, fear, apathy, curiosity, admiration, disgust, and so on. If we place tattooing as a relationship that exists between art and identity, it encourages us to think of it as a reference to one's agency and control over their own bodily presentation: "Because of the unique manner in which tattoos are produced and consumed, the act of being tattooed suggests an inherent degree of agency that is unlike the consumption of other bodily goods" (Kosut 2006, 1042). Anne, Laura, Maria, and Ra'anaa all have tattoos. (The other participants may also have tattoos but did not acknowledge them). These four participants discuss tattooing in ways that, I think, speak to how their tattoos function as representations of transformation.

94 Transforming Bodies

[Laura was showing me their tattoos, so this is written as if Laura is showing you as well.]

So, here are my tattoos: the shapes are the molecular structure of hormones. Testosterone, estrogen, and progesterone all have this basic shape. Yes. And then the colors are nonbinary pride colors. The mountains are because of my hiking obsession. I'm a photographer, and this is a representation of my home and where my where my heart lives, which I guess is Berlin. And this is the skyline. And then this is for video games. And specifically for one video game that got me through a really bad depression.

(Laura)

[Ra'anaa was also showing me their tattoos, so this is written as if Ra'anaa is showing you as well.]

I have a lot of tattoos. I love this one. And my friend gave me a tattoo of a magpie. And I also had this tattoo of like a scythe underneath it, and the scythe tattoo, the artist had called it, 'reap your own happiness.' And then my friend gave me the magpie tattoo, later, like a couple months ago, and we looked it up because she thought there is a poem about magpies, and we found there's an old nursery rhyme, that says one is for sorrow, two is for happiness, three is for blah, blah, blah, and whatever. Wait, I'll show you right now because this is fun and fresh, but so the scythe is right here and the magpies there. And I'm like, it's interesting, because like, one is for sorrow, and then to reap your own happiness and then Ekundayo [their last name] becomes happiness, which I did accidentally and I didn't even know. It's so fucking fitting.

(Ra'anaa)

[Anne was also showing me her tattoos, so this is written as if Anne is showing you as well.]

I have around 20 tattoos. So, part of my desire to get them is because I'm a skin picker. I don't even realize I'm doing it. I started getting tattoos because I wanted to hide the scars for my wedding. This was sort of my first – the one with the octopus on her. She's huge because I wanted to cover up scars for my wedding pictures. But I love it. This one, this one is badass. This makes me feel powerful. This is art. I love this stuff. Then I started getting more and it's me. This is me. It's art. It's creative. That's how I feel with the tattoos on my body. Not the dolphin – don't look at that one. *laughing* That's very 90s. I'm working on getting that covered. I do feel they're sexy, too. Whether people like them or not, I don't care. And I've had like, especially it's funny to watch my daughter's friends come around, because they're always looking at my arms. Are those tattoos? Did it hurt you? Can I get one? But so, it started as something I used to hide because of my insecurity. But then it became a *process; I love this. I want to do this for myself. It's no longer about the scars. I just love the art of it, and how it looks with my clothes and how I look with it. It makes me happy.*

(Anne)

In all three excerpts, these stories relay the role of agency and transformation as connecting to the tattoos that they have. "Contemporary members of the body modification movement who use extreme modifications in non-normative ways see themselves as taking control of their own bodies and expressing their individual identities through these practices" (DeMello 2014, 219). In terms of self-presentation, Anne's discussion is interesting because she sees her tattoos as intimately tied to sexuality. As DeMello (2014) says,

Since the 1960s, when tattooing began to move slowly from the margins of American society into the middle class, women have been using tattoos as a way to reclaim their bodies, and both men and women have been using tattooing as a way to highlight their sexuality. (217)

This chapter began with a quote from Maria saying,

My body transformations relate, of course, to my top surgery, but I also have tattoos. I have a lot of tattoos. I have a half sleeve; I have a full sleeve. And I've got one leg pretty extensively covered. So, especially in the summer, people will stop me and they'll comment on that, too.

The interactivity that tattoos provide, particularly visible ones, is an element of the transformative process that they offer. Our interactions with other people are altered by the images that appear on our flesh; they can inspire conversation, questions, or even simply stares, but these encounters are not neutral. They have impact and meaning in relation to how we identify and what it means when we opt to change our bodies in these permanent ways.
Maria goes on to say:

My tattoos are mostly fandom pieces, which is truly a part of who I am. I try to get pieces that are aesthetically pleasing and interesting. And that whatever their primary references are for me, you don't need to know that in order to be like, "That's a cool tattoo." A lot of them are from shows, books, and games that I really like, but most of them people can look at without, you know, needing a specific text to connect.

96 Transforming Bodies

Not all tattoos need to bear significant meaning, they can sometimes simply be a cool aesthetic. Kosut (2006) argues that

> [e]ven if the meanings of tattoos shift, and their present cultural currency declines or exhausts, most tattooed bodies will bear this ironic fad for the course of the life cycle. For some people, the permanence of tattoos contributes to their allure and cultural significance.
>
> *(1041)*

We All Perform

Earlier in this chapter, there is a quote from Jules saying, "When I leave that stage, it's just a performance of a less public kind. I am still me and I am still performing." What does it mean to say that we are all performing in some way? This is a challenging concept for my students when I ask them to consider how they are *doing* gender now. If gender is more of a verb than a noun, what does it mean to say you are currently doing it, even when it might escape your notice? It often feels very natural and taken for granted, but, through all the stories in this chapter, there are many intentional elements to consider when it comes to how we perform our identities and what it means to transform those performances over the course of our lives.

Jules says one other very important thing when they were talking about clothing that some of you might connect with. I leave it with you as an end to this chapter.

> *RuPaul says, "We're all born naked and the rest is drag." This might seem silly, but Mother Ru is rarely wrong. Even if we think about all of the choices we make in prepping ourselves for the day, they are all manufactured decisions based on some idea from someone else – someone we don't even know. There is nothing natural about fashion. There is nothing natural about the words I use. There is nothing natural about my hair color – ha! It's all a stage. The whole fucking world.*
>
> (Jules)

Key Terms

Body Modification – Body modification is the intentional altering of the human body or appearance.

Fashion – Fashion is the most general term and applies to any way of dressing, behaving, writing, or performing that is favored at any one time or place.

Gender Performativity – Gender performativity is the theory that gender and gender roles are elaborate social performances that we each put on in everyday life.

Questions for Reflection and Discussion

1. "All the world's a stage" is something William Shakespeare apparently once said. The participants in this chapter seem to agree with him. Do you agree with this? Why or why not?
2. Why do you think there has been such a rise in the interest of having tattoos? Do you have any? Do you plan to get any?
3. When you reflect on this chapter, do any of these ideas impact how you imagine your own gendered performances? Has it caused you to imagine the things you do to alter your body and perhaps how they could be different?

References

Benedict, Elizabeth, ed. 2015. "Introduction." In *Me, My Hair, and I: Twenty-Seven Women Untangle an Obsession*. New York: Workman.

Burney, Ellen. 2019. "Untangling the Politics of Hair." *Vogue India*. www.vogue.in/beauty/content/the-politics-of-hair-how-protest-hair-became-a-form-of-political-expression.

Butler, Judith. 2006. *Gender Trouble: Feminism and the Subversion of Identity*. London, England: Routledge.

Christel, Deborah A., and Susan C. Williams Née Dunn. 2018. "What Plus-Size Means for Plus-Size Women: A Mixed-Methods Approach." *Studies in Communication Sciences* 18 (2): 339–52. https://doi.org/10.24434/j.scoms.2018.02.009.

Davidson, Deborah. 2017. *The Tattoo Project: Commemorative Tattoos, Visual Culture, and the Digital Archive*. Toronto: Canadian Scholars Press.

DeMello, Margo. 2014. *Body Studies: An Introduction*. New York: Routledge.

Fahs, Breanne. 2022. *Unshaved: Resistance and Revolution in Women's Body Hair Politics*. Seattle: University of Washington Press.

Garland Thomson, Rosemarie. 2009. *Staring: How We Look*. New York: Oxford.

Goffman, Erving. 1959. *The Presentation of Self in Everyday Life*. Garden City, NY: Doubleday.

Golden, Marita. 2015. "My Black Hair." In *Me, My Hair, and I: Twenty-Seven Women Untangle an Obsession*, edited by Elizabeth Benedict, 19–33. New York: Workman.

Kaiser, Susan B. 2012. *Fashion and Cultural Studies*. New York: Bloomsbury.

Kannen, Victoria. 2021. *Gendered Bodies and Public Scrutiny: Women's Stories of Staring, Strangers, and Fierce Resistance*. Toronto: Women's Press.

Kosut, Mary. 2006. "An Ironic Fad: The Commodification and Consumption of Tattoos." *The Journal of Popular Culture* 39 (6): 1035–48. https://doi.org/10.1111/j.1540-5931.2006.00333.x.

Orbach, Susie. 2009. *Bodies*. New York: Picador.

Plemons, Eric. 2017. *The Look of a Woman. Facial Feminization Surgery and the Aims of Trans-Medicine*. Durham and London: Duke.

7
BODIES TRANSFORM

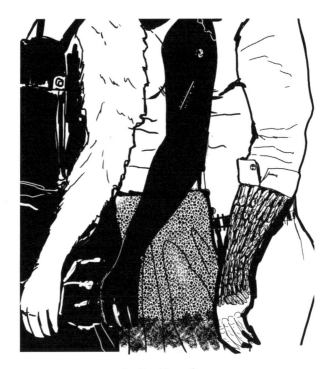

Bodies Transform

FIGURE 7.1 *I wanted the cover image, which is this image, to be both abstract and specific. On the cover, the colors are intended to catch your eye, but what these bodies represent in terms of gender is up to you. Why repost this here? Well, this is a nice way to wrap up these ideas – kinda abstract, but also familiar. What might transformation mean to these characters? How do you understand them? How might you have imagined them differently?* Note from Victoria: At the end of this chapter, there are opportunities for you to draw, write your own body story, or simply answer any of the questions you've encountered or created while reading. We hope you consider using the space!

Damian Mellin, 2024

DOI: 10.4324/9781003380061-7

> *Your body often experiences consequences of which you're not in control. It's a narrative beyond you, right?*
>
> (Hila)

> *There is so much to this story. It's hard to know where it begins and ends. I guess that it doesn't.*
>
> (Anne)

When you sit and interview people for so many hours, there is a plethora of anecdotes, important comments, and lovely observations that do not all get to make their way into a book like this. I decided that I wanted to use this chapter as a space where some of the ideas on transformation that may not have fit easily into the previous chapters get to flourish. It is my hope that by this point in the book, it is clear that listening to the stories of people who have been impacted so much by transformation, as well marginalization, dis/ability, illness, and injustice, is a meaningful form of **advocacy**. Sharing stories such as these allows us to learn from the experiences of Others, while also giving us the opportunity to reflect on our own bodies, choices, experiences, and changes. These are meaningful exercises. As such, I also asked the participants to share some advice and insight into transforming bodies for you, which seems like the perfect way for us to conclude our time together.

Bodies as Homes

In our current cultural climate, there is a lot of pushback against people who unapologetically transform, particularly when they gender transition. It seems very challenging for some people to accept that bodies and identities can change, while some other people embrace transforming bodies and identities as a matter of daily existence. This first group tends to believe that there are strict opposites. Many people like to imagine that they don't have to alter what they know to be true because they have been taught that we live in a world of binaries – healthy versus unhealthy, men versus women, straight versus gay, fat versus thin, young versus old, and so on. Then, there are ideas and theories placed on top of those binaries to help define and reinforce the binaries to make them appear to be true.

At the same time, there is a second group of people who embrace the idea of change as fundamental to who they are: desiring fluidity, transformations, questions, and journeys. "Identities, after all, are plural, open-ended, creative and transgressive. From this angle, identity is always particular, an utterly unique conditioning and construction of one's life" (Elliot 2015, 3). So, for these people, their very embodiment seems to show how bodies and identities do not exist within binaries at all. Recognizing that these contrasts

100 Transforming Bodies

exist is important because it reminds people like me that the ideas that I am sharing here could be entirely new and controversial to those who believe in strict opposites. Much like many elements of education, being open to new ideas might be a process of **unlearning**. As Laura describes, our changes and transitions can impact and alter how we know and understand our bodies:

> *And I think that having gone through gender transition initially, and having learned that I can be the person I want to be, has really changed my perspective on my own body. Having this experience has shown me how much agency I actually have over my body. And having that experience of this is continuing down the path of how I want my body to continue to change and grow. And the fact that I can actually make that happen is something that really changed my outlook and my relationship to my body, not just because of how my body changed, but also just the dynamic between me and my physical form has definitely changed through that experience of ownership in a way of not just inhabitation, but shaping my body as my home.*

I so appreciated how Laura framed the ways that our bodies are our homes, but more than that, I appreciated how Laura said the word "shaping." Our bodies may not always feel like homes to us; they may feel misaligned, not representative of who or how we want to present. But, if we consider our body stories as those *in process*, then we can shape our bodies as we go.

Interestingly, Jules also referred to their body as their home. Jules says,

> *My corporeal being is not for the faint of heart, sister. This is a temple. This is my home. No one else's. Mine. I protect it from those who might try to diminish me. When you live on the margins, you learn how to protect yourself.*

In *Exile & Pride: Disability, Queerness and Liberation* (2009), Eli Clare connects the body to home as well:

> The body as home, but only if it is understood that language too lives under the skin. I think of the words crip, queer, freak, redneck. None of these are easy words. They mark the jagged edge between self-hatred and pride, the chasm between how the dominant culture views marginalized peoples and how we view ourselves, the razor between finding home, finding our bodies, and living in exile, living on the metaphoric mountain.

(12)

As queer people, Laura and Jules are framing the experience of their changing bodies similarly to Clare (and to one another). They discuss their changing bodies within frameworks recognizing the marginalization they experience from society, but they are also grounding those changes within a safe place for them – their own bodies.

Hopefully, through all the stories shared in this book, it is clear that the journey of transformation is not one where you are first one thing and then you arrive at another – it is always a process. At times, embracing that not-quite-there part of a journey can be a challenging one. The next two sections – "Bodies as Shared" and "Bodies as In-Between Spaces" – offers some stories on how we can hold space when transformation might take both expected and unexpected twists and turns.

Bodies as Shared

A very interesting element of transformation that is often taken for granted as a normal element of embodied life is **pregnancy**. Pregnant bodies are inherently transforming, but I didn't have any participant respond who specifically wanted to talk about the story of their pregnant body. It seems as though the way I was framing transformation was seemingly speaking to those with unusual experiences, and pregnancy is not connected with that idea: "[T]he body is formed through an engagement with specific cultural regimes and so outside of this particular context the body cannot make sense or be interpretable" (Richardson and Locks 2014, 4). Hila and I ended up chatting quite a bit about the body in relation to all the elements of pregnancy that seemed relevant: being not pregnant, trying to be pregnant, actually being pregnant, and no longer being pregnant, but that was accidental. We started down a path discussing eating disorders and we happened upon an anecdote about her experience with **in vitro fertilization (IVF)**. Why do you think I had no participant explicitly contact me to discuss pregnancy? I have my suspicions as I noted earlier: it seems ordinary. As a person who was once pregnant, I can assure you, a pregnant body is not ordinary, it is definitely *extra*ordinary. Pregnancy "effectively disrupts the ordinarily stable, and largely taken-for-granted, boundary between inside and outside, person and place" (Davidson 2001, 283). This quote by Joyce Davidson (2001) is a lot to unpack. Considering a pregnant body as a representation of something that is inside and outside, while simultaneously being a person, but also a place can be a challenging idea to grasp. Traditionally, pregnant bodies are considered a natural state of being, but once we start to think about them in social ways, as the epitome of transforming bodies, then they become less straightforward.

The majority of Hila's story was about her experience with her body's shape, as discussed in Chapter 3, but another important element of her

102 Transforming Bodies

story – and many body stories – is her experience of trying to get pregnant. Pregnancy is a significant embodied change that is seemingly quite normal, but a unique and often challenging experience for those who become – or cannot become – pregnant. When I was in graduate school, I became pregnant with my daughter, and it impacted my graduate research to such an extent that I ended up publishing a paper on it in 2013 called "Pregnant, Privileged and PhDing: Exploring Embodiments in Qualitative Research" in the *Journal of Gender Studies*. I say,

> Interestingly, what became significant about my body in the process of studying identity was not my height, or even the topics that I was explicitly exploring – gender, race, or ability – rather, what was significant was my identity as a 7-month pregnant 27-year-old researcher. This pregnancy, as combined with other aspects of my identity, exposed the complexity involved in the process of interviewing and its relation to notions of social power.
>
> *(Kannen 2013, 178)*

As a quick summary, this article that I wrote is about how much my pregnant body impacted the research that I was doing because when I would be interviewing people, the subject of my pregnancy often took over. The participants would ask me questions about my body, my unborn baby, and my future career path now that I was to be a mother. Also, there were hugs. Many hugs. Once I gave birth and no longer was pregnant, there were – among other changes – no hugs at the end of the interview. What was most interesting about my publishing of this paper over ten years ago is that many people still reach out to me regarding their own experiences as researchers who get pregnant and identify with some of what I shared about touching, questions, and seemingly well-meaning but often unsettling, comments regarding pregnant bodies.

In Hila's story, I noted that she tells the story of *trying to* get pregnant. This is because her story primarily focuses on her experience with IVF. IVF is a medical procedure in which an egg (or oocyte) is fertilized outside of the body and then transferred into a uterus. She describes her experience of IVF as a medicalized, gendered reality:

> *I would feel so sick for the first 10 weeks, like unbelievably sick, then I would go off all the drugs, because you're allowed to go off the drugs for a week, and I would feel fine once everything kind of went out of your body. But then there's all these injections, and you're just like, they just send them to you the mail. And then you're supposed to do it yourself. Some of them you have to mix. This was a tough thing mentally – mixing them and administering them yourself. At home. And I remember*

Bodies Transform **103**

*being like, if I was a man, I would be in the hospital. Men would not
be expected to mix drugs and administer these kinds of medicines, you
know, injections, like several times a day to themselves and some are
time-sensitive. I firmly believe that men would not have to do this at
home. Also, it always felt like if you don't do it at this time or in this
way, then you know, everything gets fucked up and it's your fault. It's
just wild, like it is actually wild. How much responsibility is put to you
to manage the medications and to administer the medications? It's so
mentally and physically consuming. And, now that I went through successful pregnancies and I am a mom, it is such a realization of how much
all of this is mentally and physically consuming. Such a gendered reality.*

(Hila)

Hila's experience of trying to get pregnant was physically, mentally, and
emotionally challenging because of expectations, hope, loss, grief, and the
overwhelming effect that IVF treatments have to impact the changes in her
body. Hila shared her experience of going through many cycles of IVF and
how that transformed her experience of her body – as both a person and a
professor:

*I think one of the toughest things about going through IVF is not really
being able to talk about it. When I was younger, I got pregnant once
by accident from someone who I was dating. He wasn't interested, but
was fine about me having it and raising it myself. Great. And then I lost
it. And I was so shocked. Like, it just didn't cross my mind that the
pregnancy wouldn't lead to a baby. I could have miscarriage? It just
did not cross my mind. And then I realized, like, oh, I really wanted a
baby, so I should just get myself a baby. And that's when I solicited the
sperm donor. And I just thought that I don't actually have any problems
preventing me from getting pregnant. The only issue that I have is that
I don't have sperm. I started IVF with a donor. And then we froze the
embryo that we made, and then that process took so long that I ended
up meeting the person in the interim that is now my husband. Then we
started trying and I was getting pregnant all the time, but it wasn't stick-
ing. So, then we started IVF and it worked.*

*Don't get me wrong – it's great that it worked, but it's so consuming.
All consuming. There is so much I could say about the financial cost of
all of this in the States and how some was covered and some wasn't, and
I was privileged to have amazing healthcare, but I'd rather talk about
the overwhelming toll it took on my body. First of all, you have to go
to all these appointments. They're constantly looking at your uterus.*

You have an unbelievable number of days with a wand in your body! I was going at five or six in the morning, having the checks, then driving to work. I worked, like an hour away, you know, and all the while you're hiding all of this, right? You're hiding all of this from almost everyone you know. I had one colleague that was a friend, so she knew, but otherwise, I am trying to do my job while my body is going through so much that I feel like I am expected not to talk about. And then, you know, then it doesn't work. Then you go back into the grief, and then you go right back on the IVF drugs. And you know, sometimes I get upset with myself about the kind of work I produced as an academic during this time. I think, "Well, did I really publish enough?" They say you're supposed to send 10 things when you want tenure. I don't have 10 things. And it's all-consuming. Right? So first my eating disorder was all-consuming, then you have to go to therapy for fucking 10 years about it. Yeah, and you have fertility issues, which then really fucks with your body. And by you know, like I spent so long in therapy being like, you don't have to be afraid of being fat. You don't have to be afraid of your body being bigger because your body hasn't changed in twenty years. Like, oh, now it changed again. It turns out, you cannot guarantee me that my body will not change. It will. And you know, and then you got to go back to therapy about that. So, it's very . . . the fertility thing is really wild.

(Hila)

She expressed that she felt her body was both a medicalized space and (a somewhat) sad clock:

Because I found it hard every month. Once I realized I didn't get pregnant, it was sad. Even now, even though we're not actually trying to get pregnant anymore because I had both of my pregnancies from IVF, it's still sad every month when I am not pregnant. I became so used to my body making me sad. Literally every month was sad when I would get my period. I can't emotionally . . . I can't have this. And the plus? I can't not count my cycle days even now. You know, and it's like, okay, well, I know it's cycle day 12 . . . not that you asked!

(Hila)

The complexity of being pregnant, not being pregnant, and so on encompasses many elements of change. Not only do bodies change size, shape, health, but one's very personhood also changes as you could be seen as more than one person for a time, particularly in the later, often visible stages. Idealized pregnancy and post-pregnant bodies proliferate on social media, as well as expectations on diet, health, and the de-sexualization of pregnant bodies (Mayoh 2019). All these representations can be so challenging to navigate, in addition to the complexities that Hila has outlined earlier. Pregnant bodies go through so many venues of transformation, and it was important to include a nod, even if a brief one, to that effect here.

Bodies as In-Between Places

The stories here are often focused on gendered bodies because gender is a guiding principle in our lives. Other identities are always intertwining and intersecting with gender, but many of the stories here engage with elements of gender as a transformative process. There is also not one right way to do gender, to be in a body, or to understand yourself. "Some bodies avail themselves of theories of gendered fluidity and flux, play and performance. Others do not" (Plemons 2017, 16). Gender is not an element of ourselves that can be said to be done once and for all because, like all elements of identity, our understanding and experience of it is always in process.

When we consider in-between spaces, they are often referred to as **liminal** spaces. *Liminality* is an abstract term that describes the threshold of what lies in between, or on the margins of, more well-defined times or spaces. It is a space that can be disorienting, transitional, and ambiguous. A compelling element of Ari's story is a liminal experience of their gender transition, singing voice, and testosterone's impact:

> I started on testosterone (T), not because I don't like my body and I want my body to be different. It was that I wanted people to stop thinking that I'm a fucking woman. Right? It was really preventative. If people had not been seeing me all the time as a woman. I don't know that I would have gone through with taking testosterone. But it was defensive. It was preventative. And I knew that it would lead to people perceiving me as a man, which was wrong, but it was less painful than people perceiving me as a woman.
>
> The biggest worry for me about taking testosterone was the potential change that would happen to my voice.
>
> My singing is a way for me to express emotion that is unparalleled in anything else that I do. The connections I have with my fellow singers are deeper than anybody else. And I'm pretty good at singing. I was in a couple of semi-professional choirs. And, you know, I didn't make my living at it, but I got paid to do it on occasion. And so, the thing about

testosterone, and this was the kind of narratives circulating in trans com-munities, were that if you take T, your voice is going to be wrecked.

So, it's great that your voice gets lower with T, but as somebody who's really connected and identified with their voice, and my voice for me was a way I could connect with other people, I was living in a perpetual state of worry. And I knew that I would still be able to express myself, but my voice could have fallen, and then I would have to contend with the fact that it could or could not be able to do what I expected it to do anymore. I didn't think I would lose my voice. But you know, the kind of stories claim that essentially, your voice gets hoarse, it gets weak, it gets unstable, it gets much more fragile, you have much less capacity, and your voice just gets tired more quickly.

The change in my voice was that I lost a fourth at the top and I gained a fourth at the bottom, which is actually pretty small, like the overlap, and the notes I could sing before and after is huge. And I still feel very connected to the higher part of my range. And I'm super grateful that I still have it and we could go on forever to talk about that voice process. But it was a really gradual process. I wanted to do T, but there were risks to important elements of my life.

The way that Ari expresses taking testosterone connects to Clare's idea of exile. Clare (2009) says that exile

is a big word, a hard word. It implies not only loss, but a sense of alle-giance and connection – however ambivalent – to the place left behind, an attitude of mourning rather than of "good riddance." It also carries with it the sense of being pushed out, compelled to leave.

(35)

Ari's story can relate to any moment we are on the threshold of a change and we need to reflect on its importance to us and what the costs might be, but we feel compelled to make the transition regardless.

Jasmine's story also recounts her experience of shifting body sizes along-side huge social pressures to have her body shape reflect particular ideals of femininity. For her, it is a feeling of often being misaligned with the expecta-tions she feels are placed upon her:

It's challenging to figure out where you belong. We equate fitness and privilege and all of those things. We police each other. I think every step of the way, when I am looking back at my body journey, I feel like I was being policed. Whether that's internal or external, I felt like I had to fit into this rigorous box, and even when I was in my bodybuilding shows, there would be every now and then someone who would come up to me and say, 'I don't like girls with muscles.' At this point, I'm in the best shape of my life, but mentally, I'm in the worst space of my life. I look good and I know I look good because I've looked bigger and fatter and not in a good place before, so I know I fit with what I am supposed to look like. I would often get compliments from other women and men about how my body looks, but then there are those moments where I was making people feel turned off.

I literally went on stage and allowed people to judge me, but I felt so good thinking that I knew what the judgements should be. And yet, still criticism. It's this constant idea that we're never quite there – always trying to get there, but always in between. We're never gonna check every box, and we don't. I don't know how much people think about this stuff, because if they recognize the sort of dichotomies going on they can work at letting them go. But, when somebody comes along and says something about how you look, that is opposite to how you feel, you can begin to question it.

There's so many overlapping ideas of what it means to be a woman; what it means to be a thin woman; what it means to be a sexy, attractive woman. It's hard to keep them all straight. We also privilege men's bodies. We have more stores available for them. The clothing is bigger. It goes up to bigger sizes. It compensates for the expected and varying size of men. When we go into airplanes, and there's a big guy there we're like, 'Oh, I feel so bad for him!' Whereas when people see a fat woman, it is like 'Oh, my God! I hope she's not sitting next to me!' Where is the point where I cross the winning finish line? What counts as the right body for a woman? I am embracing the change in my body now, but it has been a long road.

(Jasmine)

There is so much to unpack in Jasmine's story that I want to let most of it percolate on its own, but the key piece that stays with me is the idea that when we see what we consider to be an unusual body, it often provokes some form of disconnect for the person who sees it. This is perhaps not so much because of what the bodies themselves look like but because they disrupt what form bodies people take pride in and what form they should feel ashamed about. As Garland Thomson (2009) states, "The sight of an unexpected body – that is to say, a body that does not conform to our expectations for an ordinary body – is compelling because it disorders expectations. Such disorder is at once novel and disturbing" (37). Of course, these are subjective assessments, but they have such a drastic impact on where and how people feel they fit within that narrow understanding of 'normal' that it can seem impossible to leave the threshold of 'not quite.' It takes time, learning, and acceptance to

108 Transforming Bodies

get to a place where being in-between or in-process is something desirable. For the last section of this chapter, I want to share some advice the participants have offered to you based on their transformation journeys.

Bodies Have Stories

The title of Sonya Renee Taylor's (2021) book is *The Body is Not an Apology. The Power of Radical Self-Love*, and, quite honestly, it's an amazing title. Let's pause on this: The body is not an apology. I have come to cherish the idea of not apologizing for who I am for a long time. But it took me a while to get to that place. I used to hunch my shoulders, try to shrink my tall frame, as if I was apologizing to those around me for the space that I took up. At a book talk I was giving recently, someone in the audience asked if I find writing about bodies to be healing for me. I think reading and writing are definitely elements of how we can move forward from the negative ideas we speak to ourselves (mostly because we have been exposed to negative ideas from others). I recognize that it might seem silly to include a space for you to write at the end of this book, but what if it isn't? What if you use the space to write something private and it turns out to be a moment that you needed? Your body has a story to tell. It's a low-key risk, and maybe, just maybe, it might lead somewhere cool for you.

At the beginning of this chapter, I said that I see storytelling as a place where advocacy can happen. Acknowledging the stories and experiences of other people is so important to foster compassion and empathy within the world around us. It also reminds us that we all have stories that are worthy of being told. Many of my participants, some of which have been featured the most in this book, responded to my call for participants with a caveat that went something like this: I think I might have a story to tell, but I actually don't know if my story matters enough to warrant being included. Women, non-binary, genderqueer, and other marginalized folx are so often made to feel that our stories are not worthy of taking up space or that our ideas are not going to add meaningful contributions to society. It simply isn't true, and I hope that this book conveys their importance in substantial ways.

Part of this advocacy is listening to the stories of Others who may or may not be like you, and an even greater privilege is having people who have lived through transformation share some insights with you. As such, I invited the participants to give you some advice. As Taylor (2021) says, "[h]ow we value and honor our own bodies impacts how we value and honor the bodies of others" (5). I hope that you find some pearls of wisdom in what they have to say. (I also added my own at the end!) These are people who have given considerable reflection to their body stories and here they express some of those insights:

Bodies Transform **109**

*In 2019, I went back to school [and] earned my MA [master's degree].
Yes. And now I'm defending my dissertation next week for PhD, and
I never considered doing that before I was diagnosed with cancer. And
I hadn't really thought about it, but I think that this experience could
have done that. I felt like my kids were going away to college. And I need
to do something with my life more than what I've been doing. I don't
know if my illness played into that or not? But I guess my illness affected
everything. Either way, I'm in my 50s and getting a PhD. It is never too
late to change your path.*

(Alane)

*You really need to look beneath the surface. We have to really get beyond
that first impression thing. I think that that one is really so tough. We
are more than how we look. I'd love that to be something people try
to remember and accept. I also don't want people to say "at least you
are still here" or "at least you survived cancer." I get it, but I also want
people to still see me as beautiful and worthy regardless of how I look.*

(Amelia)

*Fatphobia is a nightmare. I don't work out to lose weight anymore,
I work out to feel healthy. I feel power in not letting calorie-counting or
food preoccupation control me. I feel power in that now because before
I couldn't control that fear. I want my daughter to let go of those fears.
I want people reading this to embrace who they are and how they look
at every stage of their life. Don't waste so much time.*

(Anne)

*Just keep moving and get strong. Being strong is good at every age is
so important – inside and out. You know, it's empowering to be able to
do what you want to do as you get older. I'm in my 60s and I feel that
there's nothing like can't do. I mean, I went hiking in Nepal a few years
ago, and I can get on a bike and nothing bothers me. I have the physical
capacity to do anything I want to do. The whole emphasis on women
being skinny has puzzled me all my life. I mean, there's nothing wrong
with being strong.*

(Audrey)

*Whenever one of my friends changes pronouns, or names, I put a stop
sign in my head or slow down sign in my head. So, I give myself a note to
reflect on 'What do I need to think about?' When I'm talking about them
out loud, I just remember to slow down a little bit, not a lot, but just a little bit, so I can make sure that I'm thinking about the pronoun I'm using*

110 Transforming Bodies

and thinking about the name that I'm using. It's respectful and it's what I want people to do for me. It doesn't need to be perfect, just thoughtful.

(Haz)

We also need to remember that labels and ideas and all that stuff exist, but it's not a box you must fit into. You can have one leg in the box or whatever. So, I am trans, but I am wearing a dress right now and I am presenting as a woman. But that doesn't mean that that's the full story. Your gender doesn't have to be exactly what you've always pictured. Or like, I also struggled with whether I should identify as fat or not. Was this my box? Not quite, but I'm kind of there and I connect with a fat identity. So, I should be able to claim it. Do other people see it that way? Maybe not, but how I see it matters.

(Haz, again)

Bodies are always part of the story, you know? And in some ways that you would expect, but often in ways that you don't expect. Relationships with bodies are hard. It's hard to be in a body. But you can make it less hard, though. You can make that relationship less hard. If you have an eating disorder or if you think maybe some of the things that you're doing are just consuming your mind space, get help now. Do not under any circumstances do what I did and wait out of fear or shame to get treatment. That's a lot of years and then you don't get them back. If you're uncomfortable with your relationship to your body, get help so that you can have a better relationship, but it doesn't have to be stressful. There actually are ways to learn to at least be body-neutral. Obviously, you don't have to love your body but you don't have to hate it. I think that's a really worthwhile project to do as soon as humanly possible because, letting yourself be consumed by body preoccupation is not time well spent.

(Hila)

I think that there's probably two main things that I have learned over the course of everything is that you are worthy. It really just doesn't matter what your size is, or how other people are treating you. You're just worthy to be here. What's going on inside of you is much more important than what's happening on the outside of you. Because when I was working so hard to be so thin, I was in the worst place inside of myself that I have ever been. I was not a nice person to myself and I was not a nice person to others. I was over-consumed with something that was not worth being overconsumed with. I even landed up in the hospital so it didn't even physically make me a very healthy person. When I got help, I learned to not be afraid of food and being okay with extra weight on my body and looking at health in a different way. I internally like myself more. I take better care of myself. I am nicer to other people. I am able to put that energy that I had towards something much more exciting and much more fulfilling.

(Jasmine)

I'm not going to say any cliché bullshit, but I will say that loving yourself enough is not easy, but it's worth it. Love yourself enough to shut up the assholes that try or want to take you down. Be creative. Be flamboyant. Change it up. Life is too short to worry about the people who don't understand you and they don't need your worry. I think that is a big lesson – don't waste your worry on other people. That is energy you won't get back. I really believe that. Your body is yours and do what you want with it – even when that is really hard. Fill your own cup. Fuck, that's a cliché. Whatever! It's a good one. Haha.

(Jules)

I'm a completely open person, but not everyone is. For someone like me, I like how tall I am. I like how wide my shoulders are. I like the fact that most days, I like how testosterone has shaped my body, and then how estrogen has shaped it on top of that. I'm not just one aspect. No one is.

(Laura)

Make your body what you want and need it to be. You know, and of course, that manages to be very broad, and to encompass the spectrum of difference because people have different wants, needs and desires for their bodies. Various types of body modification and transformation can often work towards the same goal. Whether you want and need a gender presentation that differs from one the one you have now, or wanting physiological and embodied reminders of things – like tattoos – that you enjoy or that help make you who you are or even just ones that are aesthetically pleasing, all of those can be seen as moving you toward that super broad goal of being who you want to be. Embrace that.

(Maria)

For me, a big reminder is that you don't have to look disabled to be disabled. That's one major thing I've been preaching since high school. But also, I think it's important to remember to not make assumptions on how people have become or are disabled. And most people, if you ask nicely, are not afraid to answer your questions, but also don't presume that you can ask questions. I'm always been open to answering questions whenever it happens. I understand curiosity, but people can also not answer your questions and being okay with that is really important.

(Michelle)

112 Transforming Bodies

Let your freak flag fly. And do not let any stupid fucking noise in that doesn't serve you. I've just kind of got to this point where I don't give a shit about how other people think. And it's so interesting, because the second that I just started dressing for myself, wearing whatever I want, carrying myself in a confident way, everyone was like: "Wow, you look so good." They are so in love with it. Maybe it's partially being older, or it's the confidence. It really doesn't matter how other people perceive you, if you're not perceiving yourself in a way that you see yourself. For so much of my life, I would just look in the mirror and while it's me, I didn't feel it was quite right and then I'm disconnected. But the second that I realized that I can carry myself in a way where I feel comfortable, then all of a sudden, I started to attract the coolest humans around me. And the coolest shit started to happen for me. And it was really liberating to be able to put my energy towards resistance and liberation and abolishing the harmful systems, and dismantling all of these institutions that are inherently harmful. But liberation is also through carrying yourself how you want and embodying resistance through being the person that you're meant to be and by being unapologetically that.

(Ra'anaa)

I think that it's important to remember that nothing is permanent. It's okay that things change. It's okay to be happy with where you are right now. But it's also okay to close that chapter or understand that that chapter is gone, and you're going to a new phase. If you stay the same forever, then you are not growing. The things I went through were hard. So, the next thing that comes might be really hard, but I know that I have already. gotten through something hard. I've got this. I think with just that understanding, things are going to change, it's good, even if the change is bad at the time. You're never gonna stay the same. We all transform.

(Rachel)

Thinness does not equal wellness. That's a tough lesson. I've been Comparing a picture of myself when I was at my thinnest to a picture of myself now. I am still considered thin, but when I was at my thinnest, I was not well, yet people would glorify how thin I was, as if it was success. I think that it can be very hard not to comment on other people's bodies, but it's important to pause before you do to consider what it is you are commenting on and why. We don't really know how other people will feel about what are pointing out about them. Even when a comment about another person comes from a seemingly good place, it can be trouble. For example, a friend of mine recently became smaller because of weight loss and a woman in a work meeting commented on how great she looked because she was thinner. What this well-intentioned woman didn't realize is that my friend had been quite ill and it wasn't an intentional change in weight, but one due to her illness. The belief that thinness equals health or, in my case, extraordinarily tall height in women invites questions and comments, are just two examples of the ways we often talk to others about how their bodies present. My advice, if you don't know someone very, very well (and sometimes even when you do) keep your comments to the realm of "you look so happy today!" rather than something body-related.

(Victoria)

We all transform. We all change. It is my hope that you have learned and feel changed by some of what you read/heard in this book. These stories are snapshots of people's lives, but they offer so much insight into how transformation can impact us as well as those around us. Sometimes transformation can happen quickly, sometimes it can happen slowly, but it always happens. Understanding these changes as a reality of our lives and being open to learning about experiences that may differ from your own is such an important tool for being a compassionate person who cares about making the world a more accepting place to be.

Thank you for going on this journey with us.

Key Terms

Advocacy – Advocacy is defined as an activity by an individual or group that aims to influence decisions on behalf of others to create social change within political, economic, and/or social institutions.

In vitro fertilization (IVF) – IVF is a medical procedure in which an egg (or oocyte) is fertilized outside of the body and then transferred into a uterus.

Liminal – The meaning of a liminal space is of, relating to, or placed at a sensory threshold. It is a transitional or intermediate state, stage, or period.

Pregnancy – Pregnancy is the term used to describe the time period in which a fetus develops inside a womb or uterus. Pregnancy usually lasts about 40 weeks, or just over 9 months, as measured from the last menstrual period to delivery.

Unlearning – Unlearning is defined as the process of examining one's beliefs about a particular topic, concept, idea, or thought and deconstructing it to the core in order to reestablish a new belief.

Questions for Reflection and Discussion

1. What do you see as the most important lesson that this book offers to you? Is there anyone in your life who might benefit from reading a book like this? Why?

2. In Chapter 1, I introduced the idea of your body and asked: What has it been through? What has been challenging for your body to deal with? What questions have other people had for you about something related to your body? How might you imagine the ways that your body will change in the future? Also, which of these questions can you answer right away, and which might you need some time to process? Why?
3. How has your own body transformed through the process of reading this? What has changed for you – either physically or mentally considering these stories?

References

Clare, Eli. 2009. *Exile & Pride: Disability, Queerness and Liberation.* Cambridge, MA: South End.

Davidson, Joyce. 2001. "Pregnant Pauses: Agoraphobic Embodiment and the Limits of (Im)pregnability." *Gender, Place & Culture* 8 (3): 283–97. https://doi.org/10.1080/09663690120067357.

Elliot, Anthony. 2015. *Identity Troubles: An Introduction.* New York: Routledge.

Garland Thomson, Rosemarie. 2009. *Staring: How We Look.* New York: Oxford.

Kannen, Victoria. 2013. "Pregnant, Privileged and PhDing: Exploring Embodiments in Qualitative Research." *Journal of Gender Studies* 22 (2): 178–91.

Mayoh, Joanne. 2019. "Perfect Pregnancy? Pregnant Bodies, Digital Leisure and the Presentation of Self." *Leisure Studies* 38(2): 204–17. https://doi.org/10.1080/02614367.2018.1562492.

Plemons, Eric. 2017. *The Look of a Woman. Facial Feminization Surgery and the Aims of Trans-Medicine.* Durham and London: Duke.

Richardson, Niall, and Adam Locks. 2014. *Body Studies: The Basics.* London: Routledge.

Taylor, Sonya Renee. 2021. *The Body is Not an Apology. The Power of Radical Self-Love.* 2nd ed. Oakland, CA: Berrett-Koehler Publishers.

My Body Story

As this is the last chapter of the book, I thought I would give you a space to craft your own body story. Here are some questions for reflection to get you started:

- How would you describe your body? What is something that you love about your body? (See what I did there? Some people will immediately think about something negative but try to avoid that urge.) I'll even ask it again, just in case: What is something that you **love** about your body?
- In what ways has your body transformed in the last five years? Ten years? How would you describe those transformations to someone who doesn't know you?
- Have you ever had someone come up to you in public to ask you something about how you look? What did they say? How do you respond? How did it make you feel? Why was this experience memorable for you?
- Are there any assumptions that people make of you based on how you look?
- Have you altered your body because of other people's comments?
- How does your offline identity differ from your online identity?
- Have you considered your gender, race, class, sexuality, age, dis/ability, and so on before reading this book? Has this book altered these understandings at all? How might that impact your own body story?

116 Transforming Bodies

Bodies Transform **117**

118 Transforming Bodies

Body Art

Here, you could use this space to draw yourself, have someone else draw you, or draw one of the participants in the way that you envisioned them. Or just create a doodle. Being creative and making space for creativity is never a waste of time! This is your space – do what you want with it.

INDEX

2SLGBTQIA+ 32–34, 70, 81

ability 61, 66
ableism 54, 60
activism 3, 12, 16, 21
ADHD *see* attention deficit hyperactivity disorder
advocacy 10, 21, 99, 108
AFAB *see* assigned female at birth
age 4, 10, 53–54, 56–58, 65, 66, 74, 89, 109, 115; aging 16, 56–58, 86
ageism 56–60, 66
agender 5, 17, 18, 22, 32, 33
age stratification 56–57, 66
AMAB *see* assigned male at birth
androgynous 32, 33
anti racism 10
asexual 32, 33
assigned female at birth 17, 33, 51
assigned male at birth 17, 51
attention deficit hyperactivity disorder 60

bald 57; baldness 86, 87
bigender 33
biological identity 5
bisexual 32, 33
Black Lives Matter 31, 79
Blackness 12, 79
BLM *see* Black Lives Matter
bodybuilding 11, 23, 107
body modification 8, 12, 93, 95, 96, 111
body neutrality 15, 50

body positivity 15, 43–44, 50
body project 8
body shape 15, 24, 37, 38, 43, 85, 106
body size 3, 9, 24, 33, 36, 40, 42, 106
body story 16, 43, 98, 115; body stories 2, 13, 17, 86, 100, 102, 108
boobs 38, 47–49
breast(s) 26–27, 33, 34, 38, 46–52, 57, 92
breast augmentation 46, 48–49, 50
breast cancer 9, 26–27, 48, 57
breast reduction 46
Butler, Judith 84–85

chest(s) 15, 27, 38–39, 46–49, 52
cis 11, 24, 49; cisgender 5, 13, 17, 22, 33, 38, 49, 51, 66, 71
cishet 58, 66
class 22, 24–25, 33, 34, 40, 81, 95, 115
colonial 29, 78, 87
colonization 29, 33, 69
constructionist approach 4, 17
COVID-19 pandemic 64, 84, 91
Crenshaw, Kimberlé 25, 31

DeMello, Margo 5, 28, 32, 93, 95
diaspora/diasporic 29, 33, 79
disability 12, 26, 54–62, 66
dis/ability 3, 16, 53, 54, 60–62, 65, 66, 99, 115
drag 54, 61, 69, 80, 85, 89, 96; drag king 83; drag queen 11, 38

120 Index

eating disorder 9, 11, 23, 38, 40, 44, 62, 101, 104, 110
embodied transformation 3, 6, 17, 19, 22, 24, 26, 30–31, 65
embodiment 3, 8, 12, 17, 18, 29, 42, 99, 102
empowerment 12, 43, 87
estrogen 26, 33, 51, 94, 111

facial feminization surgery 75, 85
fashion 4, 6, 16, 53, 81, 84, 89–92, 96
fat 23, 40–46, 50–51, 99, 107, 110; fatness 11, 41–42, 44–45
fatphobia 41, 43, 51, 109
feminism 10, 17, 84; feminist 7, 13, 17, 25, 30, 40, 54, 70
FFS *see* facial feminization surgery
folx 71, 73, 81, 108

Garland Thomson, Rosemarie 37, 55, 60–61, 88, 107
gay 32, 33, 99
gender affirmation 15, 27, 46–47, 49, 51
gender dysphoria 46, 51, 81
genderfluid 5, 10, 18, 22, 32, 33
gender identity 17, 18, 46, 51, 57, 69, 71, 72, 78, 85
genderless 5, 18
gender-nonconforming 48, 70
gender performativity 16, 84, 97
genderqueer 10, 23, 33, 74, 108
Goffman, Erving 24, 39, 84

hair 4, 6, 9, 16, 28, 51, 57, 81, 84–88, 93, 96
heteronormative 37, 51
heterosexism 30
heterosexual 5, 27, 51, 66, 69
homophobia 25, 33
hormone replacement therapy 48, 51
HRT *see* hormone replacement therapy

inclusive language 70, 81
intersectionality 15, 20, 21, 24–25, 30–31, 33–34
intersex 32, 33, 51
IVF *see* in-vitro fertilization
in-vitro fertilization 101–4, 113

lesbian 32, 33, 88
liminal 105, 113

mastectomy 26–27, 34, 36, 46, 48
McIntosh, Peggy 30
mental health 42, 48, 71, 73–74

non-binary 33, 52, 70, 94
normal 23, 26, 30, 34, 38–40, 55, 63, 66, 77, 92, 101–2

onomastics 77, 81
oppress 23, 25, 32, 34, 56, 71
Orbach, Susie 4, 8, 41, 84–85, 93
Other 23–24, 28–29, 34, 39

pansexual 33
post-traumatic stress disorder 62
power dynamic 32, 73
pregnancy 33, 42, 101–5, 113
privilege 7–8, 18, 23, 25, 34, 42, 43, 45, 46, 54, 56, 71, 102, 103, 106–8; white privilege 11, 28, 30, 31
pronouns 10–12, 14, 24, 70–73, 75, 81, 109
PTSD *see* post-traumatic stress disorder

qualitative methodology 7, 18, 42, 102
queer 10, 12, 14, 21–25, 31–34, 40, 70–72, 74, 79, 100–1, 108
questioning 32, 33, 79

race 3, 4, 8, 15, 21, 24, 25, 27–34, 54, 56, 57, 81, 87, 102, 115; racialized 23, 24, 29, 40, 55, 87
racial identity 29
racism 25, 28–30, 34
representation 4, 14, 15, 39, 44, 54, 55, 66, 93–94, 101, 104

sex 17, 18, 25, 32–34, 51
sexism 17, 18, 25, 30
sexuality 3, 4, 9, 12, 15, 20, 21–22, 25, 27, 31–34, 49, 86, 95, 115
shame 41–43, 50, 89, 107, 110
social power 32, 102
stigma 24, 34, 39, 42, 51
storytelling 6–8, 13, 62, 93, 108
straight 5, 44, 45, 51, 69, 71, 99

tattoo 4, 9, 12, 16, 36, 81, 83–84, 88, 93–96, 111
testosterone 48, 51, 94, 105–6, 111
thin 10, 23, 37–38, 40–43, 84, 90, 99, 107, 110, 112; thinness 11, 37–38, 41, 87, 112–13

top surgery 12, 46–48, 52, 84, 95
trans 7, 10, 11, 14, 20, 46–49, 51, 61, 69, 73, 75–77, 106, 110; transgender 5, 17, 18, 32, 33, 46–47, 51, 52, 70, 73–74, 81, 91
transformation 2–4, 6–11, 13, 14–17, 19, 22–23, 25–28, 30–31, 33, 40–42, 57, 65, 79–80, 84, 89, 93, 95, 98–99, 101, 105, 108, 111, 113, 115

transition 2, 11, 12, 15, 16, 18, 21–24, 26, 43, 51, 57, 73, 75–77, 86, 99–100, 105–6, 113
transphobia 77, 81

unlearning 100, 113

whiteness 25, 30

youngism 58, 66

Printed in the United States
by Baker & Taylor Publisher Services